THE WORLD
OF
PSYCHIC RESEARCH

The World of Psychic Research

By
HEREWARD CARRINGTON

Director of the American Psychical Institute

South Brunswick
New York: A. S. Barnes and Company, Inc.
London: Thomas Yoseloff, Ltd

Originally published as *The Invisible World*.
© 1946 by Hereward Carrington
New material in this edition © 1973 by
A. S. Barnes and Co., Inc.
New edition published 1973.
Library of Congress Catalogue Card Number: 72-6371

A. S. Barnes and Co., Inc.
Cranbury, New Jersey 08512

Thomas Yoseloff, Ltd
108 New Bond Street
London W1Y OQX, England

ISBN 0-498-01299-9

Printed in the United States of America

CONTENTS

	Foreword to the Second Edition	
	Preface	7
I.	The New Spiritual Awakening	9
II.	Haunted Houses	17
III.	Eusapia Palladino	27
IV.	The Greatest Mental Medium of All Time—Mrs. Piper	41
V.	Laboratory Investigations in Psychic Phenomena	52
VI.	Trumpet Mediums	64
VII.	The Intra-Atomic Quantity	94
VIII.	Experiments I Should Like Tried at My Own Death	105
IX.	Poltergeist Phenomena	110
X.	How Spirit Pictures Are Faked	121
XI.	Psychic Photographs	127
XII.	The Visions and Voices of Jeanne D'Arc	135
XIII.	The Problem of the Mind-Body Relation	140
XIV.	Free Will and Determinism in the Light of Psychic Phenomena	149
XV.	Yoga and Magic	162
	Appendix	186
	Index	189

FOREWORD TO THE SECOND EDITION

AFTER ALMOST THREE centuries of Enlightenment-dominated thought, we in the West are experiencing a resurgence of a nonsensationalist epistemology. Such varied phenomena as the prevalence of drug use, the wide interest in transcendental meditation and "cosmic consciousness," the revival of satanism, and the spreading scientific study of extrasensory perception, all point to a growing, if still undefined, conviction among specialists as well as interested amateurs that there may be more to human knowledge than that which is transmitted by the five senses. Astrology—in both the careful work of official societies and the vulgarized mumbo-jumbo of the popular press—has never enjoyed a wider vogue; and the immense popularity of novels (later films) like *Rosemary's Baby* and *The Exorcist* also implies—notwithstanding the puerile, merely naughty character of much modern satanism—a reawakening of mental states long held anathematic or simply absurd.

Partly this can be explained away as a reaction to the dominant sense of anomie which seems to infuse most of the Western societies in this post-Nietzschean, atomic world. In so far as they are merely reactive, the claims of the astrologers and meditators that they have found The Answer can be ignored as special pleading. But not all the forms of the nonsensationalist revival are suspect in this manner; specifically, the scientific claims of the psychics can not, in the face of still undigested evidence, be blithely ignored.

The new interest in the world of psychic research is no fantastic excrescence. The lunatic fringe have of course always been awed by visions of a world beyond the physical and temporal one: those who need balm for frightened minds generally find it. But when professional scientists at Duke and UCLA and Maimonides Medical Center—to pass over the several Soviet scientists now engaged in psychical research—devote time and money to investigations of extrasensory phenomena and "supernormal" states of consciousness, it is something else again. When a thinker with the generous and precise intelligence of a Colin Wilson devotes a huge and serious text to *The Occult*, it is fair to say that the field merits serious attention.

And it is getting some. Belatedly, the claims of the psychics are being critically examined. In 1969 the American Association for the Advancement of Science accepted the Parapsychological Association as an affiliate, thus sanctioning what was already, in the world outside the academies, a *fait accompli*.

Science's interest in the extrasensory world is a relatively new development, however. The world of academic science has not infrequently been resistant to innovation: Galileo and, in this century, the much maligned Immanuel Velikovsky are only the major cases in point. It is always refreshing, then, to find an avid researcher, ignored or vilified by the academies, who keeps the steady courage needed to continue his work in spite of established doctrine and with only his own conviction as guide.

Hereward Carrington was one of these. Over a half century in which psychic research was frequently relegated by the conventional wisdom to the same scrapheap as phrenology, card-reading, mesmerism, and augury—those disciplines most easily dismissed as panaceas for the spiritually hungry—Dr. Carrington maintained a steady and sober approach to the subject. Often denatured and misrepresented by charlatans and fools who were also, inevitably, attracted to it, psychic research became, in his capable hands, an eminently reasonable way of investigating the world within and without us. He, and others like him, used the empirical Enlightenment methodology to refute the sensationalist world the Enlightenment had created. Just as Hume had, in a purely verbal way, turned Lockean sensationalism on its head by forcing it out to its own logical *reductio,* solipsism, so Carrington and his contemporary fellow advocates for psychic research forced a reexamination of the nature of human existence by using the experimental method of modern science to question science's own accepted axioms.

Perhaps he was a good researcher and perhaps not. Surely many would prefer to call him a mystic or a dreamer rather than a scientist. But that issue can not be decided until more facts are in. What is interesting about men like Carrington, from the point of view of the historical evolution of ideas, is not their dreaminess but their deep-driven rationality. Paradoxically, the mesmerist is an only half-weaned child of the Enlightenment. Mesmer himself, by most accounts an honest if misguided man, was not an eccentric aberration in an otherwise sane century, but the very type of the eighteenth-century natural philosopher: avidly curious, energetic, sublimely confident in the power of the human mind to interpret and control, he was far closer in temperament to his contemporary Ben Franklin (who investigated him for the French government) than to the moody spiritualists of a period with whom he has often been equated.

With as much rationality as, and more humility than, Mesmer, Carrington strove to understand the physical world in a wider way than the way of modern science. He was a sensible man—neither the Faustian megalomaniac of medieval legend nor the doddy bewhiskered professor which our tenuously democratic nation has often put forward as the archetype of the intellectual. "Divorced from reality," the standard jibe of the illiterate, was not a phrase which anyone could reasonably apply to him. His firm English education, his careful philosophic temper, and his eager curiosity combined to form a sensitive mind of great balance and insight, which produced, over the span of fifty years, more than a hundred books and a thousand articles on psychic and other scientific subjects. He tackled what he called the "invisible world" with a detached and yet avid interest. At the age of nineteen he joined the Society of Psychical Research, then only seventeen years old itself; later he was to found and direct the American Psychical Institute. In 1940 and 1941 he hosted a popular radio program called "Who Knows?" on which, like the *philosophes* of an earlier day, he sought to extend to others the strange new knowledge he was acquiring. He constantly urged laboratory investigation of psychic phenomena, and to this end he both collaborated with C.T.R. Wilson on adapting his ionization chamber for the measurement of possible astral projection, and offered himself as a subject for postmortem psychical experimentation. He was a man who, avoiding the Barnumesque frivolity which is endemic to the field, approached his *idée fixe* with a constant benevolent clearheadedness.

His progenitors, therefore, are not the hoary starstruck alchemists, not the magi or the yogis or the mystics, but those well-disposed, confidently excited investigators of his own heritage, the amateur scientists of the eighteenth century: Franklin, Jefferson, Faraday, Tull. His long dead countrymen, who opened doors simply by virtue of their untrained and inexhaustible fervor, are the fitting exemplars against which to measure the achievements of a man who, two centuries later, ironically shook their conclusions by adopting their method.

That is the striking paradox of psychical research today. Science, by its own laws, is being forced toward what would previously have been called an unscientific attitude. For modern psychical research suggests a far more complicated world than that of the sensationalist epistemology. An interesting article by Samuel Moffat on the "psychic boom" in the 1973 *Britannica Yearbook of Science and the Future* suggests that there is a good probability that human beings are in contact with each other in ways that can not be accounted for with a merely sensationalist physics; so the work of both Soviet and Western scientists implies. If this is true, then science, if it remains scrupulously true to its own axioms, should move closer to the immaterial, the shifting and evanescent, the invisible world which classical, post-Newtonian science had always thought it had to deny. After Einstein and Heisenberg, physics moves ever closer to the occult. Science approaches the conditions of poetry, of music, of God.

This is probably more of a jump than the sober Dr. Carrington would have made. He was like Bertrand Russell a dedicated and humane agnostic, and he spoke not of God but of a spiritual awakening, and of the "One Great Mind." But who knows where that is likely to lead? To the gypsies' world of "other" knowledge, to what the parapsychologists call "psi capacity," to what Colin Wilson calls the dark side of the moon, to a finally impenetrable and majestic future? The future, Carrington was convinced, "is always fan shaped." His cautiousness is understandable. His sense of fairness, his intelligence, finally his obedience to what he felt was Reason, commend themselves to a new generation of readers.

His curious little book, the record, as the original subtitle suggested, of "experiences out of a lifetime of psychical research," is neither apologetic nor strident, but a sane recounting by a convinced man of a few of the more memorable of his experiences. As one would expect from a nostalgic mélange, its broadly enthusiastic tone occasionally slips into a most unscientific effusiveness, and his generally well-chosen examples are sometimes spiced with merely jolting trivia. Here too he is akin to the eighteenth-century philosophers; he could escape no better than they the inherent ironies of the popular, democratic disseminator of serious material, and met with no less ambivalence the twin exigencies of publicity and fact.

Yet his discourse never becomes blather; even in his most effusive moments he retains a critical perspective. Even when the prose is shot through with the traditional cloying ecstacy of the nineteenth-century medium (which is seldom), the relation has depth and conviction. He was a man who believed what he was saying. Never descending to the level of publicist for parlor tricksters, he keeps his readers constantly aware of the gravity, no less than the intoxication, of his theme.

What is finally most engaging about his reflective compendium is the sincerity with which he adapted a scientific attitude to his own peculiar interest. With less brilliance than Freud, perhaps finally with no more validity, but with the same perseverance, he vigorously championed his infant science, staying diligently on his own track until—as Thoreau promises—the world came around to him. Of course parapsychology has not attained the eminence which modern psychologists grant to psychoanalyis

—partly because the *Traumdeutung* precedes J. B. Rhine's early experiments by more than thirty years— and as a result little recognition has been given its early apologists like Carrington. He is also still relatively obscure because, in spite of the magnitude of his *oeuvre*, he lacked both the dogged negative capability peculiar to graduate students, and the carnival panache of a Kreskin. Without his early spreading of interest in psychical research, however, it is doubtful that the Rhines' 1934 monograph *Extra-Sensory Perception* would have made quite the splash it did. Carrington was in this sense both herald and bulldog for the academic parapsychologists. Parapsychology still has a great deal of experimentation to do before it establishes itself as undebatably a science, but when and if that occurs, we may expect to see the conviction and intensity of this industrious man receive the appreciation they have long deserved.

—Thaddeus Tuleja

PREFACE

AFTER HAVING DEVOTED more than forty-five years to psychical research, one might perhaps be expected to have arrived at certain definite conclusions upon the subject. In a certain sense I feel that I have done so; yet such conclusions are still fluid and elastic and subject to change. I feel quite assured of the *reality* of psychic phenomena; the *facts* as such are, in my estimation, undoubted. Supernormal phenomena *occur;* they are facts in nature. But as to the second problem—the explanation of such occurrences—I can only fall back upon a sort of agnosticism. Facts and the interpretation of facts are two very different matters; so that, while I feel assured as to the reality of the main phenomena, their final elucidation still escapes me. That is why we need psychic laboratories—to study such manifestations and discover, if possible, their underlying laws and mechanisms. A well-equipped and endowed psychic laboratory is, I believe, one of the prime needs of our time.

Some of the chapters composing this book have appeared in *The Journal* of the American Society for Psychical Research and elsewhere, and my thanks are due for permission to utilize them here. Some of the material is new, and is published in this book for the first time. I can only hope that it contains some useful suggestions.

I wish to acknowledge here my great indebtedness to Dr. F. I. Regardie, for material furnished in connection with the chapter on *Yoga and Magic,* and to Dawn Edwards, for her help in preparing the manuscript for publication.

H. C.

Hollywood, Calif.

I

THE NEW SPIRITUAL AWAKENING

IN THE WORLD OF TODAY we have a "psychology without a soul." Spiritual philosophy has been replaced by mechanism—but a *bad* mechanism which is not even consistent within itself. The human body and the human mind are held to be mere machines in which anything truly psychic is lacking. Mechanism has been transformed by many scientific men into a religion.

And yet everyone knows that no machine runs itself. A printing press or a typewriter, beautifully intricate though they are, would produce nothing were they not guided and controlled by the hands and minds of men. No machine by itself accomplishes intelligent work; it would rot from disuse if not controlled by human guidance. And yet another machine—the human body—is supposed not only to run itself, but to initiate original ideas and to perpetuate other machines like itself *ad infinitum*. The dogma of mechanism, carried to its logical conclusion, ends in absurdity.

The refusal of modern savants to perceive this self-contradiction, and grant the existence in man of some active, conscious principle, is an anachronism for which it is difficult to account. One can only assume that the triumphs of physical science, during the past century, have blinded them to obvious realities.

It is true that we live in a skeptical, cynical age, in which ultimate realities are ignored and only appearances "count." "But," as Socrates remarked shortly before drinking the hemlock, "just because I am about to die does not entitle us to use bad logic." Religious beliefs and dogmas are rapidly vanishing, it is true, and the younger generation is growing up in the firm conviction that death is the end of all things. Men and women of today require concrete facts upon which to build some philosophy of life, and in their absence refuse to accept the bygone faiths of yesteryear. They demand specific evidence for anything they may believe. They want *facts*. Are any such facts available?

Yes, such facts *are* available—in the form of certain psychic phenomena. This has been perceived most clearly by Jules Romains, who stated in his book *I Believe:*

> ... Science may one day find itself confronted by results so coherent and conclusive, achieved through methods still roughly described as "psychic" that it will be impossible for it to regard these results, as it now does, as null and void.... Once the most important results of psychic experimentation are proved and officially recognized as "truths," positive science will be challenged within its own province.... When this happens I hold that human reason will have to discard very nearly all its current ideas about time, space, causality, the determinism of phenomena, human free will, the nature of the soul and the cosmos....

The mind and spirit of man are greater and more potent than the physical organism through which they function; rather, they "overflow" it in all dimensions, as Dr. Alexis Carrel stated in his *Man, the Unknown*. There are faculties or powers within man enabling him to acquire information and knowledge not obtained through the five senses—which faculties are seemingly not the result of mere terrene evolution.

These higher powers of mind and spirit are not, it is

THE NEW SPIRITUAL AWAKENING 11

true, universally active or manifest. If they were there would be no doubt as to their actuality. But they have been noted in times of stress, or in the presence of certain peculiarly endowed individuals known as sensitives or psychics, who are probably as rare as geniuses in any other sphere of human activity. They constitute the exceptions, not the rule. But is there not an old saying that "the exception proves the rule"?

A violin built by one of the Old Masters is valuable and hard to find, and many are the worthless imitations which have been sold by unscrupulous dealers in their stead. Yet an imitation implies a genuine, a copy an original. And it is equally true that, despite the illusion, fraud and superstition which have unfortunately associated themselves with this subject, there are genuine psychic phenomena which are as yet unexplained by modern science, and which have tentatively been relegated into a class by themselves, designated the supernormal.

The experiments recently undertaken by Dr. J. B. Rhine, of Duke University, alone show this. They have proved (or rather *re*-proved) the actuality of extra sensory perception: the reality of such powers as telepathy and clairvoyance. They have shown us that space and time may be transcended, that man is not a mere animal reacting to his environment, but that he possesses within him powers inexplicable by mechanistic science. Man must represent a duality rather than a unity, a spiritual being no less than a material structure.

Attempts which have been made to draw very tempting analogies between the radio and possible brain waves have completely broken down. Seemingly no such physical analogies are possible. No centers or areas have been found in the human brain capable of sending or receiving such mental messages, nor have they the necessary kinetic energy to do so. Instrumental tests have failed to reveal the actuality of any such cerebral radiations. All energies known to us diminish in intensity according to the law of inverse squares. No such limitation is shown in telepathic messages which are seemingly conveyed with as great intensity from Bombay to London as they are from one room to another. Radio waves are purely mechanical in their nature, and convey neither symbolism nor inner meaning. All these we find in telepathic transfer.

No. Physical analogies fail us here. The conveyance of thought from one mind to another is not mechanical in nature. Far less so can be those clairvoyant visions in which are often perceived distant events actually transpiring as though present and real; nor those glimpses of the unlived future which nevertheless occur precisely as foreseen.

And yet, if these things be true and remain inexplicable by mechanistic science, how may we account for them? Surely only by admitting that man is more than the machine he animates, and that there is in truth some superphysical world in which man dwells, and in which he lives and moves and has his being.

This receives added confirmation from the great mass of recorded psychic manifestations which have been noted throughout all history, in every portion of the civilized and uncivilized world, and which are being reported today from drawing rooms in London and Paris and New York. They are not remote and infrequent, as many seem to think, but of relative frequency. It has in fact been estimated that at least one person in every ten has experienced at one time or another in his life some form of psychic manifestation. If this be true, there are in the United States alone more than *twelve million persons* who have experienced some variety of psychic manifestation! How,

THE NEW SPIRITUAL AWAKENING 13

in the face of this, can it be said that such phenomena are negligible or non-existent?

Many such manifestations cluster about death in a curious but significant manner. Phantasmal appearances—apparitions—have been seen at the precise moment of some individual's death, when that death may have been sudden and many hundreds of miles distant from the locale of its perception. Such experiences are relatively common. Years ago the Society for Psychical Research published its famous *Census of Hallucinations,* in which it was shown that such occurrences took place far more frequently than could be accounted for by chance. This conclusion was based upon some 30,000 replies received in answer to a questionnaire, and the report, after a most careful and painstaking analysis, concludes with these words:

Between deaths and apparitions of the dying person a connection exists which is not due to chance alone. This we hold as a proved fact.

Again, if it *be* a fact, how profoundly must this conclusion affect psychological science! "Thought is a function of the brain" we have had instilled into us. Were this true, thought could no more exist as an "independent variable" in the world, as William James called it, than a shadow could exist without some opaque body casting it. Yet such facts undoubtedly exist, and the day will come when science must ultimately recognize and grapple with them.

The human brain, instead of being a thought-creating mechanism, may in truth be a thought-transmitting instrument, permitting the flow through it of spiritual or mental energy. It is highly possible that one of the chief functions of the human brain is to temper and regulate the flow of thought to its suitable speed upon this material plane.

All energy remains forever invisible and intangible to us. We should never be enabled to perceive the presence of energy did not that energy play upon matter. We perceive its effects upon matter, which alone checks and records it. Radio waves would remain forever unperceived did we not possess the suitable instrument capable of catching and transforming them. The heat radiated by a fire, due to increased molecular motion, would not be sensed unless some material body (a wall, a thermometer or your own body) were interposed to register it. The ether is teeming with unsensed, invisible energies which only become sensible to us when they play upon and influence matter.

Similarly, may it not be that the human brain is an instrument especially designed and constructed to detect mental and psychic energies, and that all space about us is filled with mental or spiritual forces, normally insensible to us, but which may become manifest through the instrumentality of certain peculiarly endowed organic receptors?

There are many scientific men, as we know, who believe that this is so; they believe that they have received actual evidence of this fact—evidence painfully and cautiously collected over a number of years. They assert that they have actually received messages from such a mental sphere, separated from our own only by the thinnest of veils. Certainly the positive evidence of such men should have more weight with us than the negative evidence of those who have *not* obtained, or attempted to obtain, such evidence! The testimony of an otherwise trustworthy man who asserts that he has performed a certain experiment in physics is assuredly worth more than the *a priori* assertion of another that it "cannot be done." And the same should apply to psychic experimentation.

The stream of consciousness known to us in life as a definite personality resides always in its own mental world; dreams and reverie prove to us how true this is. To psychic investigators it becomes a question of *fact* as to whether this consciousness continues to live in its mental world, insensible to us save during its occasional contacts with matter. Proofs of identity—of the memories, ideas, associations and points of view of such a personality—would go far toward establishing its persistence. It is such proofs which the psychical researcher seeks, and, according to the testimony of many, has found.

It is certain that such proof of our persistence would give a meaning to life which it would otherwise lack. Why are we here? What is the object of our existence? Every thoughtful person must have asked himself such questions at one time or another in his career. Nature has taken millions upon millions of years to perfect a living, human consciousness. To what end? If death be the finale of that consciousness, we can see no valid reason for its gradual emergence and perfection. Perfecting a thing merely to destroy it does not reveal common sense. But if there be some persistence, then one can perhaps begin to see the reason for its being. Proof of human survival would furnish such evidence, and it may be pointed out that, from the purely scientific point of view, such proof would constitute the *only* valid evidence we possess.

Thus it is that upon these very psychic phenomena—ridiculed and despised though they may be—a whole new spiritual philosophy may be built, a cosmic viewpoint which would be impossible in their absence. That is why so many of us regard this new, this "coming science," as so vital, and why the late William E. Gladstone remarked that "psychical research is the most important work being done in the world today—by far the most important."

And in this he is by no means alone. When Roger W. Babson asked the late Charles P. Steinmetz, "What line of research will, in your opinion, see the greatest development within the next fifty years?" Steinmetz answered:

The greatest discoveries will be along spiritual lines. Here is a force which history clearly teaches has been the greatest power in the development of man and history. Yet we have played with it and have never seriously studied it as we have the physical forces. . . . Some day people will learn that material things do not bring happiness and are of little use in making men and women creative and powerful. Then the scientists of the world will turn their laboratories over to the study of spiritual forces . . . which field as yet has hardly been scratched. When that day comes the world will see more advancement in one generation than it has in the past four.

There are many among us who feel that one of the prime and urgent needs of our time is the endowment and equipment of such laboratories, suitable for the scientific investigation of psychic phenomena in all their varied aspects.

The past century was one of material progress. May we not hope that the coming years will see the investigation, by science, of these supersensible, psychical manifestations? Rightly understood and interpreted, they may furnish us with the keys to many of the enigmas of life, and prove to us that mankind is indeed one great spiritual brotherhood, encompassed by the One Great Mind.

II

HAUNTED HOUSES

WRITING OF HAUNTED HOUSES in the *Story of Psychic Science,* I said: "Experiences in such houses are not limited to visual phenomena ... for, in addition to the figures seen, sounds, footsteps, raps, whisperings, and so forth, may be heard; the inhabitants may feel touches, smell curious odors, or experience unaccountable emotional experiences. Further, many of these phenomena may be of a physical order—in which case, however, they may be said to fall under the heading of 'poltergeist' manifestations. . . ."

Two important facts should not be lost sight of in discussing such curiosities as haunted houses. In the first place there is nothing superstitious about investigating them. Either curious phenomena occur within them, or they do not. If they do, it is the task of psychical investigators to study and record them. This has been done, in many instances, in a perfectly calm, cool, judicial manner. Attempts have been made to obtain permanent records of these visual and auditory phenomena, by means of suitable instruments, and to observe what happens in a purely scientific spirit. Occasionally fraud has been unearthed— practical jokes and trickery; often normal causes have been discovered, which sufficiently explain the reported occurrences. Fear, superstition, suggestion, expectancy, hallucination, all play their part. But these explanations are all familiar to psychical investigators, and have been taken into due consideration by them, whenever called upon to investigate a case of this character. As Miss X. remarked in her *Essays in Psychical Research:*

If, on the one hand, recent systematic inquiry lends us some help in *explaining* a ghost, on the other hand it makes it the more possible to preserve a reputation for sanity, without being obliged to *explain him away.* We now have several possible hypotheses other than lying, indigestion, insanity, a morbid state of health, rats, bats, owls, hot water pipes, bell wires, a snail on the window, the wind in the chimney, vibration, ordinary sounds misinterpreted, or the result of fear and expectation. At the same time it is impossible to emphasize too strongly the absolute duty of every ghost-seer to examine every one of these hypotheses, and fifty others which his friends will undoubtedly suggest, with the utmost care and conscientious scrupulosity, before allowing it to pass into history that he has "seen a ghost."

I myself have had considerable experience in every one of the types of so-called haunted houses mentioned above. On the one hand I have seen practical jokes and fraudulent phenomena being produced (consciously), and instances where similar manifestations were seemingly brought about by some tricky and mischievous split-off portion of the personality. There have been humorous cases; instances distinctly malign and pathological, and cases where nothing happened at all. I have witnessed "poltergeist" phenomena, both genuine and fraudulent. Such well-attested cases now run into the hundreds. One of the most recent and striking of such accounts is that by Harry Price, in his book *The Most Haunted House in England,* in which the testimony of more than one hundred first-hand witnesses is summarized.*

Aside from the purely negative investigations of my own—the narration of which would only prove tedious—

---
* Since the above was written, the first-hand testimony of more than 50 additional witnesses has been secured.

HAUNTED HOUSES

I have, on several occasions, witnessed highly curious and inexplicable phenomena in haunted houses. One of the most striking of these was a house which I investigated some years ago in company with my wife and a small group of fellow researchers, and which I recorded informally at the time as follows:

On the night of August 13, 1937, a party of seven of us spent the night in a reputed "haunted house," situated some fifty miles from New York City. I had heard of the house from a friend of mine who knew the summer tenant. He had merely told me that the latter had been compelled to move back to the city in the middle of July because neither he nor his wife could secure uninterrupted nights of sleep, and that their servants had all left in consequence of the haunting. (He had rented the house until the first of October. He thus abandoned it some two and a half months before he had been obliged to.) We knew nothing more about the house than this, except that "noises" had been repeatedly heard.

Our party of seven visited the house on the night in question. The group consisted of the former occupant, two of his friends, two friends of our own, my wife and myself. We also brought with us a dog which had lived in the house while it was occupied, and which, according to reports, had behaved in an extraordinary manner on several occasions.

Arriving at the house, we found it dark and locked-up. The tenant had some difficulty in entering and turning on the lights. This he finally succeeded in doing, however, and we could then see that the house was spacious and well-appointed, and that everything had been left intact.

I suggested to the owner that, before hearing anything about the house and its history, it would be a good idea to explore it first of all from cellar to attic, to see that no practical jokers were hidden anywhere, and that no cats, bats, rats, mice, or what-not were present to account for the disturbances. To this he readily consented, and lighted the house from top to bottom.

Examination of the cellar and the ground floor revealed nothing unusual. On the second floor, however, two or three of us sensed something strange in one of the middle bedrooms. This feeling was quite intangible, but was definitely present, and seemed to be associated with an old bureau standing against one wall. (The noises had been heard by Mr. X. and his wife from the large bedroom on the side of the house.)

Walking along the hall, we came to a door which had escaped our attention the first time we had passed it.

"Where does this lead?" I asked.

"To the servants' quarters," Mr. X. replied. "Would you like to go up there?"

"By all means," I said, opening the door.

Glancing up, I could see that the top floor was brilliantly lighted, and that a steep flight of stairs lay just ahead of me. Leading the way, with the others close behind me, I ascended the stairs, and made a sharp turn to the right, finding myself confronted by a series of small rooms.

The instant I did so, I felt as though a vital blow had been delivered to my solar plexus. My forehead broke out into profuse perspiration, my head swam, and I had difficulty in swallowing. It was a most extraordinary sensation, definitely physiological, and unlike anything I had ever experienced before. A feeling of terror and panic seized me, and for the moment I had the utmost difficulty in preventing myself from turning and fleeing down the stairs! Vaguely I remember saying aloud:

"Very powerful! Very powerful!"

My wife, who was just behind me, had taken a step or two forward. She was just exclaiming, "Oh, what cute little rooms!" when the next moment she was crying, "No! No!" and raced down the steep flight of stairs like a scared rabbit! (She had not run up or down stairs for more than two years because of an injury to her back, but she flew down the stairs and past those coming up after her without even seeing or touching them!)

May I say, just here, that both my wife and myself are old-time investigators, quite unemotional and thoroughly accustomed to psychic manifestations of all kinds? My wife is a keen, cautious observer, who has sat with many mediums and exposed many frauds. I myself have done the same, and also participated in the Palladino séances, where I believed genuine phenomena were occurring, remaining quite unperturbed when "materialized" hands were pulling me about, passing their fingers through my hair, and so forth. All that time I was dictating to the stenographer precisely how I was controlling the medium —how her hands, feet and legs were being held—as our report on these sittings will show. I remained throughout quite calm and cool, as I have at innumerable séances and investigations since. But in the present instance the reaction was most intense, and almost more physiological than psychological. It was distinctly a bodily and emotional reaction—accompanied, I must confess, by a momentary mental panic and sensation of terror such as I have never known before.

Two or three of those following me had by this time reached the upper floor, and I called out a few times to my wife. Hearing no response I descended the stairs to the lower floor, to see if she had fainted or was ill. I found her sitting on the porch, breathing deeply and slowly collecting her scattered faculties. She assured me that she was all right, and would come up again in a few moments. Her first reaction had been to get into the fresh air.

Leaving her, I ascended the stairs and found the others filing down from the upper floor. Every one of them had experienced the same sensation to a greater or lesser degree. My friend G. B. had likewise experienced the utmost difficulty in swallowing, and tears were running down his face as though he were weeping copiously. All the others were likewise affected.

Having no professional medium with us, we decided to sit for a time in the front bedroom on the second floor, to see if any sounds could be heard, or phenomena of any kind noted. We accordingly arranged ourselves in a sort of circle, prepared the camera and flashlight bulbs, and turned out the lights.

We sat thus for perhaps an hour, during which time nothing visible manifested itself, and (aside from some dubious thumps on the ground floor) nothing unusual was heard. The distinct feeling of a presence was however sensed by two or three of the party. (Personally I did not feel this.)

I should say here that the two friends of the late tenant —men-about-town—had looked upon the whole expedition as a sort of lark, and had brought with them a bottle of Scotch and a bottle of gin, intending to have an amusing evening. Every half hour or so they would go down to the kitchen and mix themselves a stiff drink. It is interesting to note that these cynics experienced the same sensations as the others, and that they likewise reported difficulty in swallowing, tears running from their eyes, cold perspiration on the forehead, and other physical symptoms as did the rest of the circle.

After sitting for an hour or so with no concrete results, we decided to sit in the upper room, where the original powerful "influence" had been felt. Accordingly, we ascended the stairs—but this time not a sensation of any kind was to be felt! The room seemed absolutely clear of all influences, clean, pure and normal. It felt just like any of the other rooms. What I had previously described as a heavy, malign gas instead of a normal atmosphere was no longer there. Nothing unusual was to be sensed by any of us, and a brief sitting in the room produced no results or untoward sensations whatever.

After our original inspection of the house, and our first violent reactions, the former tenant had told us its history, disclosing for the first time the fact that a suicide had actually been committed on the upper floor, and that these rooms were thought to be the "seat" of the haunting. We had known nothing of this on our first trip, purposely asking for no information concerning the history of the house until we had explored it.

The dog, which on the first occasion had positively refused to go with us into the upper story, ran up the stairs quite naturally the second time, wagging his tail, prying into all the corners and behaving as any normal dog would. When we had tried to coax him upstairs the first time, he had growled, planted his feet before him, and refused to go forward a step. The hair on his back had stood up like that on a cat; and he behaved, in short, very much as dogs are supposed to behave in the presence of ghostly phenomena. In the present instance, however, it was factual, and I saw it with my own eyes.

It was by this time past five o'clock and getting light, so we decided to call a halt and return on another occasion, bringing with us a medium, as well as apparatus for recording possible sounds, for testing the air in the upper rooms, and so forth. Unfortunately, "the best-laid plans. . . ." One of the friends of the tenant "talked," and a brief note appeared in the papers a day or so later, which the owner of the house saw and read. As a result, he positively refused to allow us to visit the house again, and our most persuasive powers proved of no avail.

One of the most curious cases of a haunted house I have come across was one which I investigated some years ago, in Astoria, Long Island. It is a long story, which I must summarize briefly.

One morning a young man called upon me in a very excited state of mind. He told me that he was living in a house in Astoria, and that he had not only heard footsteps stamping up and down the stairs at night, but that he had, on several occasions, seen a white figure, which had even lain down on the bed beside him, so that he could feel its weight, and also the springs of the bed tremble. When he had turned up the light, however, there was nothing there.

In addition to this, he had received a series of alleged "communications" from the spirit of an old man, who had lived in that house about half a century before, as well as from other visitants. These communications stated that there was gold (valued at several million dollars) buried under the house!

Greatly excited by this, my young friend had begun to dig, and, when my wife and I went over to visit him, we found the cellar filled with earth and rocks, which he had dug up, and a hole more than thirty feet deep which he had evacuated. So far no treasure had been discovered, but he was anxious to know if I could help him in any way—particularly in solving the mystery of the ghost.

I spent several nights in the haunted house, but saw

and heard nothing of interest during my visits there. In order to check his story, however, I took with me, on three occasions, amateur and professional mediums, to see what their impressions would be. Needless to say they were told nothing as to the house, or its history.

The mediums were never permitted to go downstairs until *after* the sitting, and they knew nothing of any digging operations. I had rather come to the conclusion that the buried treasure was a pure fantasy, and rather hoped that these mediums would say, "There is no treasure here; stop your digging!"

Instead of this, however, they one and all agreed that there *was* a treasure buried under the house, and two of them drew diagrams of an alleged tunnel, near which the buried treasure lay, which had led, many years before, to an old Dutch church, about a quarter of a mile away. This was curious, since none of these mediums knew one another, and no one knew of any such tunnel.

This seeming confirmation naturally stimulated the owner of the house to more intense efforts, so that he spent nearly all his waking hours, both day and night, digging. The entire cellar was filled with rocks and earth which he had excavated. He entirely neglected his business, and worked frantically.

The upshot of this bizarre story is something of an anti-climax. After weeks of digging, no treasure had been found, and the authorities somehow got wind of his activities. One morning they visited the house, and stated that he was endangering its foundations. The poor man was compelled to fill in the immense hole he had so laboriously dug, and all ghostly manifestations ceased. Soon after this, I understand, he moved from the house, and I have heard nothing from him since.

One strange occurrence, however, *did* develop. Inquiries revealed the fact that an old Dutch church had actually stood upon the spot indicated, but that it had been demolished in 1883. This our young friend (an uneducated Sicilian) certainly had no means of knowing. Much of the information given by the mediums was certainly supernormal, inasmuch as they had made statements which were subsequently verified, and had drawn almost identical diagrams of passages, excavations, rooms, and so forth, which they had never seen, but which subsequent measurements proved to be correct!

III

EUSAPIA PALLADINO

OUTSTANDING AS AMONG the most vivid and extraordinary experiences of my life, I must count my séances with the remarkable Neapolitan medium, Eusapia Palladino. Illiterate, hardly able to sign her own name, she nevertheless possessed powers of a unique character, powers which for many years baffled the scientific men of Europe.

Attention had first been drawn to her about 1890, when Professor Lombroso obtained a series of sittings with her. For many years thereafter, she gave séances for scientific groups in Paris, London, St. Petersburg, Turin, Genoa, Milan, and many other cities in Europe. A committee of eminent men sat with her for four years in Paris, and it was here also that Professor Flammarion studied her at length. An enormous literature had sprung up about her, and scores of books and articles had appeared dealing with her phenomenal mediumship.

In 1908 a committee was appointed by the British Society for Psychical Research to go to Naples and obtain a series of séances on its behalf. This committee consisted of the Hon. Everard Feilding, Mr. W. W. Baggally and myself. All of us were well known as critics and skeptics of physical phenomena generally. During the course of our many years' investigations, we had never yet encountered any manifestations (obtained under fraud-proof conditions) which seemed to us conclusive. We were all amateur magicians and had exposed many fake mediums in the past. The Society felt, therefore, that if we brought in a positive report, it would be good evidence indeed that Eusapia possessed genuine powers of no mean order.

We visited Naples, stayed there several weeks, and had a long series of sittings with this medium, during the course of which we became firmly convinced of the supernormal nature of her manifestations. The following year (1909) I brought Eusapia to America, and a further series was held in New York.

Eusapia Palladino was primarily a physical medium—that is, but few mental phenomena were noted. Objects moved about in her presence without anyone touching them; raps of tremendous power were heard; lights appeared; musical instruments were played upon—no visible fingers touching the strings. Finally, so-called materializations took place, in which "bits of bodies" were formed, and again disintegrated, while we were watching them, leaving no trace behind. All these things happened while the medium was sitting securely held, hand and foot, and usually with light enough to enable us to perceive everything in the room fairly clearly.

Eusapia would give her séances anywhere—in a private house, in the laboratory of a university—wherever she was requested to sit. Often she would be carefully searched before the sitting, but nothing of a suspicious nature was ever found upon her. Then she would take her place at the séance table, which was merely an ordinary wooden table rather lighter than most, while several other sitters would seat themselves about it also. The person seated to her right would hold her right hand, foot and knee, while the person seated to her left would similarly control her limbs on that side. The séances all began in brilliant white light.

Behind her was erected a small cabinet, which consisted of an enclosed space, made by hanging two black curtains across one corner of the room. In this cabinet a small table was usually placed, and on this rested various small musical instruments—the property of the sitters. It should be emphasized, however, that Eusapia never sat *in* the cabinet, but always in front of it, in the circle itself. The back of her chair was usually about a foot from the cabinet curtains.

Now, in bright light, with her hands, feet and knees securely held, the table would begin to move, tilt and oscillate. Many people have obtained table tippings, and if these had been all, no particular attention would have been paid them. But, after several such tiltings, the séance table would then rise completely off the floor—that is, all four legs off the ground, and remain thus suspended in space for a number of seconds.

I have seen scores and hundreds of such levitations, and I am as assured of their reality as I am of any other facts in life. Many times, while the table was in the air, we would pass a string or a fine wire up and down, between her body and the table, showing no physical connection of any kind. These levitations have been obtained when a sitter has been underneath the table, holding both the medium's feet in his hands, while *her* hands were completely removed from it, and everyone could see perfectly clearly that she was not touching it at any point. There seemed to be a curious elastic resistance while the table was in the air, as though it were suspended on rubbers; then this would suddenly be released, and the table would fall with a crash to the floor.

I have seen the table rise three feet and more from the floor during her séances, and have had it levitate while I myself have been kneeling upon it—the medium sitting motionless in her chair, hands and feet securely held.

After these table-liftings, rappings would be heard, in the cabinet and on the séance table itself. Often these were of a remarkable character. For instance, Eusapia would knock four times on the top of the table with her own knuckles, and then hold her hand above it, at a distance of about six inches. About three seconds later, faint raps, exactly imitating those made by her, would be heard in the wood, as though they were a sort of echo—only delayed in their reply!

About this time, five knocks would be heard, which was a signal for less light. The bright light would then be turned off, and a dimmer one substituted.* Even in this, however, everything could be clearly seen, including the medium. Now, the instruments in the cabinet would be heard moving about, and finally one or more of them would float out into the séance room, continually playing. If it were the mandolin, the strings would be strummed while it was floating in the air; if the bell, this would be rung violently before being thrown to the floor.

---

*Objection has often been made to darkness, as a prerequisite for spiritualistic phenomena. I cannot discuss this question at the length it deserves in a brief footnote, beyond pointing out the fact that many delicate physical and biological energies can only manifest themselves in darkness, and are destroyed by light; and that many historic phenomena (such as the so-called "miracles" in the New Testament) were similarly reported to have taken place in darkness and semi-darkness. I drew attention to this fact in my book, *Loaves and Fishes,* and the Rev. Edward M. Duff and Dr. Thomas G. Allen have also done so, in their book *Psychical Research and the Gospel Miracles.* Thus: Lazarus was raised in the darkness of the cave or tomb; Jairus' daughter was raised by dim lamplight; the feeding of the multitude was "in the evening"; Jesus walked on the water in the dark of the night; the demoniac was cured in dim light; the stilling of the tempest was under similar conditions; when the multitude fell down, at Gethsemane, this was during the dark of the night, and so on. Many analogous cases could be quoted, in which similar conditions were deemed necessary for the production of certain supernormal physical phenomena.

The latter part of the sitting would usually be devoted to obtaining materialization phenomena, and here hands, heads and "bits of bodies" would form in space—hands firm and solid enough to push and pull the sitters out of their chairs, or grasp them with a firm touch. The fingers and thumbs of such hands could often be clearly distinguished, and they remained visible while performing their actions. And bear in mind that, during all this time, the medium remained securely held, hand and foot, and visible in the red light which was permitted at such times.

These hands were very curious. Sometimes they would be large, sometimes small. Sometimes they would be white, sometimes black, and sometimes invisible altogether. Yet they were solid and substantial, and had every appearance of being true physiological structures for the time being. The skin, hair and nails could be clearly felt during the brief period of their existence, and on more than one occasion I myself have held a hand such as this in my grasp, and had it slowly dissolve as I was holding it. It was *not* pulled away, but melted within my hand, and was gone. This is not, of course, a unique experience, as Sir Oliver Lodge, Sir William Crookes, and many other psychic investigators have reported precisely the same thing.

Mind you, both before and since that time I have seen innumerable so-called materialization séances, which were complete frauds, and I had no difficulty whatever in detecting them. As previously stated, I have been an amateur magician all my life, and know the tricks of the trade pretty well. One book of mine, in fact, *The Physical Phenomena of Spiritualism,* is devoted almost entirely to an exposé of the trick methods employed by fraudulent mediums. But, despite all this, I remain quite convinced that we saw in the presence of Eusapia Palladino genuine materializations of "bits of bodies" and other equally remarkable phenomena of an undoubtedly supernormal nature.

It is true that Eusapia resorted to trickery at times, and in this she was caught, both by ourselves and others. Her method of trickery consisted in the substitution of one hand for two, and the production of phenomena with the free hand. Nearly every group of scientific investigators had detected and described this method of trickery. Yet every one of them had emerged convinced of her genuine powers! Why, it may be asked, should she ever resort to trickery if she could produce genuine manifestations such as I have described? Is it not possible that all her phenomena might have been due to trickery, only undetected?

It is difficult to reply to this objection in a few words. But I can best answer it, perhaps, by citing a typical instance which throws light upon her peculiar psychology—and if a medium felt and thought like other people she wouldn't be a medium!

One day I took the famous magician Howard Thurston to see Eusapia. On the way there I had said to him:

"Now, Thurston, it is quite possible that Eusapia will try to trick you at first—just to see if she can. But don't make a fuss about it immediately; just let her see by your manner that you are not satisfied. She will soon settle down, and show you something really remarkable."

Sure enough, when we had taken our places at the table, Eusapia tilted it, inserted one toe under it and up went the table! Thurston glanced at me, but I merely smiled, shook my head, and said:

"Not good, Eusapia."

She thereupon smiled also, settled down in her chair, went into a light trance, and soon produced a series of perfectly magnificent genuine levitations, which so convinced Thurston that he came out in the papers the next day with a thousand-dollar challenge to any magician who could produce table levitations under the same conditions as he had seen them in her presence. The challenge was never accepted.

So here we have an instance of the fraudulent and genuine combined. The mischievous, impish self of the medium trying to "pull something," just for fun, and when she saw that she could not get away with it with impunity, she then produced the genuine article. I have seen more or less the same thing happen over and over again, and know that, while she occasionally tricked, she was also capable of producing amazing genuine phenomena which have never been explained.

Let me narrate two or three incidents that occurred at her séances, which deeply impressed me at the time, and which could not possibly have been fraudulently produced by the medium, even supposing that she had both hands and both feet free. The materialized hand which melted in mine was one of these incidents, but I shall mention a few more.

Eusapia had a deep affection for Professor Lombroso, whom she regarded as a sort of father, and whenever his name was mentioned she would invariably dissolve into tears. But, at one of our sittings, Eusapia said, quite spontaneously:

"Now, if you are all very good tonight, Lombroso may materialize!"

As a matter of fact, Lombroso did *not* materialize, nor did anyone else, but a most curious and striking phenomenon occurred, which is almost unique in psychic annals. As the séance progressed, there formed over the center of the séance table what I can only describe as a sort of psychic water-spout—a whirlpool of invisible energy, felt by everyone at the table, and affecting them so much that several of the sitters had to leave the table and go to the window to get some fresh air. As one receded from the table, this power became less and less noticeable, and as one approached it, the force became stronger and stronger, until it was well-nigh overwhelming. Nothing could be seen, nothing heard, but over the center of that table a power was operative, sensed by everyone present, which was most impressive and indicative of the reality of the invisible.

On another occasion, Eusapia asked me to go into the cabinet behind her, to replace the small table which had been thrown out onto the floor. I picked up the small table and entered the curtained recess, which was quite dark, of course, but still light enough to enable me to see the other side of the table I was holding, and to see quite clearly that no physical person was in the cabinet with me. Yet the moment I placed the table on the floor, it rose up under my hands and pressed against me. I again replaced it, and again it rose. Finally, this developed into a sort of tug-of-war between myself and the invisible influence manipulating the table on the other side. The force—whatever it was—was eventually strong enough to throw both the table and myself out of the cabinet altogether, so that we landed on the floor of the room outside! All this time, it must be remembered, the medium was seated outside the cabinet, held hand and foot by two skeptical controllers, and visible in the dim light which illumined the room.

On still another occasion, one of the gentlemen present suddenly exclaimed that the cigar case, in his inner coat pocket, had been removed by invisible fingers, and a moment later we all saw it reposing upon the top of the séance table. Then, as we were looking at it, it seemed suddenly to become doubled; it looked as though there were *two* cigar cases where there had formerly been only one! But this was an illusion. What had actually happened was that the leather case had been pulled apart, the top sliding off the lower portion, so that the two halves were now lying side by side. Then, a moment later, this sitter cried out that a cigar had been placed in his mouth by those same invisible fingers. He held it between his teeth for a few seconds, then replaced it in the cigar case.

Bear in mind that the tabletop was of light pine wood, and that any dark and opaque object held over the table could be *seen* immediately, dim as the light was at the time. If, therefore, the medium had removed one of her hands from the control and handled the cigar case with it, her hand and arm would instantly have been seen against the background of the light wood. But although we were all looking at the case intently, nothing of the sort was seen; so that it would have been utterly impossible for the medium to have handled the cigar case, even if her hands had been free. This was really a very striking phenomenon, small though it was, since it was observed under such excellent conditions of control.

I have mentioned the fact that the materialized hands were sometimes small and sometimes large. When the sitters were grasped and nearly pulled out of their chairs, they usually described the hands touching them as extremely large ones, having a powerful grip. But, in the following instance, the hand was very small and most delicate in its general appearance.

During one of the New York séances Eusapia suggested that (in addition to holding her as usual) we tie her hands and feet to the hands and feet of her controllers by means of short pieces of rope. This was done.

During the latter part of the sitting, when phenomena were in full swing, a tiny hand was seen to emerge over the top of the séance table and begin to untie the knots on the ropes binding her to her controllers. It took several seconds for this untying process to be completed, and when the right wrist had been untied the rope was coiled up and thrown at one of the sitters, striking him on the chest. The hand then went over and untied the left wrist, likewise coiling up the rope and throwing it out into the séance room.

The medium said: "I'm sorry; it is not my fault; tie me up again!" So her hands were re-tied to the wrists of her right and left hand controllers; and a *second* time the little hand untied the knots and removed the ropes. After this no attempt was made to fasten them again.

Bear in mind that all this was done while both hands of the medium were held visibly upon the table by two separate controllers, who were ascertaining at the time that they were really holding the hands of the medium, and not dummy hands, and tracing her arms to the shoulders to make sure that these members really belonged to her! The untying process, as I have said, took some considerable time—ample time for them to observe and verify all that was going on. They reported that they were undoubtedly holding the medium's hands, and of course her head was visible throughout.

The hand which untied these knots was white and small, as I have said, and was enclosed at the wrist in a sleeve of black material, which was visible as far as the elbow—and nothing beyond! The edge of the black sleeve terminated in a small white lace cuff, which was turned backward onto the sleeve itself. The dress which the medium was wearing had no lace cuff. This fact was observed very carefully at the time, both by myself and by others, who were all looking at the hand intently. Its manipulations were intelligent and sprightly.

The two gentlemen who were holding or controlling the hands of the medium at the time were Mr. Frank Tilford on one side and Mr. Daniel Frohman on the other—both practical, shrewd men of affairs, who were unlikely to be taken in by any petty trickery, and who were completely bowled over by what they had seen. It was certainly one of the most spectacular manifestations I have ever witnessed.

Those of my readers who happened to see the motion picture *Topper Takes a Holiday* will remember the incident of the decanter which rose in the air by itself, pouring out a glass of liquid into a tumbler similarly suspended in space. Of course this was done by means of trick photography, and was not intended to be taken seriously. But it is interesting to note that precisely this same thing was noted by Sir Oliver Lodge and others in séances with Eusapia Palladino years ago. They also saw a decanter raised into the air and pour out its contents into a suspended glass. So it is possible that many of the occurrences noted in fairy stories are really based upon actual happenings—psychic phenomena which had been noted and which were utilized by the narrator in the telling of his tale.

But to return to Eusapia. The phenomena witnessed in her presence were for the most part physical, though an intelligence was certainly behind them, manipulating the invisible energies involved in their production. We psychical researchers do not believe of course that when an object is moved without contact, this has been brought about by a spirit which runs around the room like a chicken, producing phenomena. No, we believe that a *mechanism* is involved, and we want to know what that mechanism is: this is why we study these phenomena in psychic laboratories.

What seemingly happens is that a form of unknown energy or invisible substance issues from the body of the medium, capable of affecting and molding matter in its immediate environment. At times this is invisible; at other times it takes form and becomes more or less solid, when we have instances of the formation of so-called ectoplasm. It is this semi-material substance which moves matter and even shapes it into different forms.

This energy-like substance issues from various parts of the medium's body, but especially from her fingertips, her solar plexus and the sexual organs—though it can be emitted elsewhere. It represents a psychic force, as yet unknown to science, but now being studied by scientific men as part and parcel of supernormal biology.

It is this energy-like substance, then, which is probably responsible for most of the phenomena noted in the immediate vicinity of the medium. But this is in turn directed by a mind of some sort: and the next question is—whose mind? Is it that of the medium or that of some extraneous spiritual entity?

The answer to this question is not easily given. Certainly many of the phenomena are controlled by the medium herself, since they are under her own volition. For instance, I have often heard Eusapia say, "Now, I shall move that stool," and, placing her hand a few inches above it, the stool moved—though there was no visible connection between the two.

In studying Eusapia's phenomena, then, I was led to these conclusions: that they may roughly be divided into three categories. In the first, certain manifestations were under the control of the conscious mind of the medium. She willed a certain thing to happen, and it did.

Second, the medium passed into trance, in which state

EUSAPIA PALLADINO

her conscious mind was no longer active. In this state the phenomena seemed to be directed by her subconscious mind, as though she were dreaming a certain thing, and this dream actually found expression in the outer world. It was as though a dog dreamed of catching a rabbit, and the dream was so vivid that a living rabbit was actually caught and killed!

But thirdly, we have cases (in deeper trance) in which the subconscious mind of the medium seems also to be superseded, and replaced by a mind altogether different from her own—an independent mind, having ideas and volitions entirely different from those of the medium.

These were the most striking and convincing of all her phenomena—and also the most rare. I have seen manifestations of this type on only a few occasions, while witnessing hundreds capable of being explained by the power of the medium herself. Here, as in so many other instances, we seem to have an inter-blending of the power of the medium herself and an external power imparted from without.

Scientific investigators of Eusapia's phenomena have attempted to explain even her most marvelous manifestations without recourse to this hypothesis. Even materialized hands they attempt to explain by means of "naturalistic" theories. What they suggest is something like this: that, just as the sculptor can mold clay by means of his material hands into various shapes, so the dynamic will of the entranced medium may similarly mold in space the semi-material emanation issuing from her own body, causing it to take the form of hands, heads and various parts of a body. They would constitute, on this theory, a variety of objectified thought-forms.

This theory is ingenious and may be all very well so far as it goes. But there are cases on record which are hard to account for on this view. For instance, at one séance given in Genoa, a complete form materialized, which was recognized by the sitters, and spoke in a low voice *in Genoese dialect*—which Eusapia did not know. Such cases certainly seem to indicate that, in some instances at least, an external spiritual being is actually involved in the production of the phenomena.

But it is certain that they have a biological basis; that is, that they are in any case dependent upon the physical body of the medium for their production. And, this being so, it is obvious that there is great need to study such phenomena in a properly equipped laboratory, fitted up with every contrivance calculated to measure, register and record these mysterious phenomena. That is why some of us have been urging for many years the setting up of such a laboratory—which is certainly one of the prime needs of our time. In it experiments could be undertaken, calculated to throw more light upon the real nature of man than all other scientific laboratories in the world combined!

Eusapia Palladino is no longer with us. She died more than twenty-five years ago. But other physical mediums have come to the fore, and some of these have been subjected to careful scientific investigation. In studying such manifestations we enter a realm of mystery; the borderland between spirit and matter. We approach the essence of life itself. It is a fascinating study, and I for one cannot but feel that the importance of such phenomena is very great—placing almost within our hands the Key to the enigmas of life and mind. They partially lift the veil from the enigmatic face of Nature, and, in the words of Sir William Crookes:

> Veil after veil we have lifted, and her face grows more beautiful, august and wond'rous with every barrier that is withdrawn!

IV

THE GREATEST MENTAL MEDIUM OF ALL TIME—MRS. PIPER

A LITTLE MORE than half a century ago, a young woman attended a private demonstration of magnetic healing in company with several of her friends. Little did she suspect the momentous upshot of that chance visit. For it was while the demonstration was in progress that she went into trance, remaining totally unconscious for some time. When she regained consciousness she found her friends clustered about her, pale-faced, and heard from their lips that she had been entranced and that, while in that condition, she had made a number of statements regarding them and their friends and relatives which she could not possibly have known. She discovered that she was a medium! Mrs. Leonore E. Piper was launched, all unwittingly, on her lifelong career as a psychic.

It was not for some years, however, that the attention of the scientific world was drawn to her extraordinary phenomena, and then in a curious and roundabout manner. The maidservant of Professor William James attended some sittings and reported the case to Mrs. James, who in turn told him. A few séances convinced him that Mrs. Piper did indeed possess extraordinary mental powers, and a short time later he turned Mrs. Piper over to Dr. Richard Hodgson, then secretary of the Society for Psychical Research, who studied her minutely for more than twenty years.

Dr. Hodgson, who had exposed many fraudulent mediums, began as a great skeptic. He had Leonore Piper shadowed by detectives, and, subsequently, all her correspondence was checked in order to see whether or not she obtained any knowledge of her sitters by normal means. Becoming convinced that such was not the case, he settled down to the serious study of her mediumship, and ended by becoming completely convinced not only of the truth of her manifestations, but also a convinced spiritualist. He believed that those who had died spoke and wrote through her.

At no time did Mrs. Piper obtain any physical phenomena; she merely passed into trance, very deep trance, and various personalities spoke through her mouth. Later on they wrote by means of her hand. The first of these was a young Indian girl and a French doctor, giving his name as Phinuit. Later this control was replaced by a group of controls who called themselves Imperator, Rector, Doctor, Prudens, and so forth. They were the same controls who had previously manifested themselves through another famous medium in England—William Stainton Moses.

Most of Leonore Piper's life was spent in Boston, though she visited England on several occasions, where she was studied by Sir Oliver Lodge, Dr. Walter Leaf, Mrs. Henry Sidgwick, and others. All of these became convinced, as had James and Hodgson before them, that Mrs. Piper possessed extraordinary powers, and many of them also ended by becoming convinced spiritualists.

Mrs. Piper would sit at a table, a pile of cushions before her. She would then gradually pass into trance, in which state she was impervious to pain and was unconscious of everything that happened around her. Then her head would fall forward upon the cushions, nose and mouth arranged so that she could breathe. The right hand

THE GREATEST MENTAL MEDIUM 43

and arm would then reach out, and a pencil would be placed in the hand. Automatic writing would then proceed, and the communications were thus obtained.

It was not that the writing itself was any miracle; it was the *content* of the message—what the writing *said*. For in these trance states Mrs. Piper would give names, dates and facts of all kinds which she certainly did not know and had no means of finding out. As James expressed it, in his *Psychology,* she was in possession of knowledge which she could not have acquired "by the normal use of her eyes and ears and wits."

In this country Professor James H. Hyslop had a number of sittings with this medium, as well as many other scientific men. I had a series of sittings with Mrs. Piper nearly forty years ago—which I still remember vividly. In them my mother and father purported to communicate, as well as Dr. Hodgson, who had then recently passed over. The details of these sittings I have published since in my *Psychology: in the Light of Psychic Phenomena* (pp. 77-114).

To illustrate the care used by the early investigators, I will cite one example. When Professor Hyslop obtained his first sittings, the arrangements were all made by Dr. Hodgson, and Mrs. Piper had no idea as to who her sitter was to be. It was in the days before automobiles, so Professor Hyslop drove up to the house in a closed carriage, wearing a black mask, which completely concealed his face. Hodgson went to the window and waved for him to come in. He did so, tiptoeing across the room and taking his place in a chair behind Mrs. Piper.

Throughout this entire sitting he never uttered a word. All the talking was done by Dr. Hodgson. Before Mrs. Piper came out of trance, Hyslop left the room, entered his cab and was driven away. Even had the medium been in a normal state, and her eyes open, she could not have seen the sitter; and even if she had seen him, she would only have observed a silent, masked man whose identity was unknown. This procedure was followed during all the initial sittings.

Yet during these sittings Professor Hyslop's name was given, the names of many members of his family, coming from the small town of Xenia, Ohio, and so much detailed family history that it took Hyslop over six months of continuous correspondence to verify all the material told him during the sittings.

Where did this knowledge come from? Here was a woman asleep in North Boston, telling of events which had occurred seventy years ago in the midwest, where she had never been. She certainly never obtained this information by means of her normal senses. Much of it referred to memories of those long dead, who claimed to be present, communicating this material. If it did not emanate from that source, whence did it come?

Here is a problem for science—the science of the future, the coming science. It is a crying shame that psychologists today, for the most part, merely ignore and ridicule such facts, instead of investigating them and trying to understand them. For, on any theory, we are confronted with a problem of gigantic magnitude.

Hundreds of people who have sat with Mrs. Piper have become convinced that they have talked with their dead relatives and friends through her, and that a future life has been proved thereby. No mere generalities were given, but specific facts, which were often verified only with difficulty. All the appearances were that Mrs. Piper's soul was in some manner removed from her body during the trance state, and somehow replaced by another spiritual entity, who then succeeded in communicating through her. The thoughts, memories and personalities of those who had gone before were identified in this manner.

One of the best communicators was G. P., who was in real life "George Pelham."* He not only wrote himself, but helped many others to come through, and for years proved a most useful collaborator. He and Hodgson had many intimate talks together.

The main problem in the case of Leonore Piper, and all similar cases, was to identify the communicator, and this can only be done by proving personal identity. By this I mean that John Doe in life had a certain individuality of his own, and possessed certain viewpoints, ideas, memories, and so forth, which were personal and essentially his own. Because of these he *was* John Doe. Now the personality of man after death is said to be essentially the same as before, so that Doe would continue to be the same person. If, therefore, we could get in touch with him, through the instrumentality of some living mechanism (a medium) and talk to him, he should be able to identify himself by giving certain memories and facts about himself which only he would be able to know. If we got enough of these, we should be likely to say to ourselves, "Sure enough, that's John Doe! Only *he* would know those things!"

That is the sort of evidence required to prove survival, and that is the sort of evidence which has been received in such quantities through Mrs. Piper. She has certainly done a great work in proving survival to scientific men. She has provided scientific evidence instead of merely emphasizing the necessity for revelation and faith.

It must not be thought, however, that this process of communication is an easy one. Every indication seems to prove, on the other hand, that it is most difficult and la-

*This name is itself a pseudonym.

borious. Let us try and imagine some of the difficulties which might be involved in attempting communication such as this.

You are a spiritual being and have learned to use or manipulate your own body and brain through years of constant effort. Even then your control of it is by no means perfect. Now, suppose that you were suddenly transposed into *another* living body and had to use *that* body to express your thoughts and ideas. You would doubtless find all sorts of impediments and difficulties which you little suspected. That body would have little tricks and automatic processes of its own, which would tend to express themselves without your volition, and you might find yourself saying and doing things which you never intended to. Doubtless this is exactly what happens when a spiritual entity controls a medium's body from the other side.

Then, too, you would have the medium's subconscious mind with which to contend, a portion of which is always left behind, so to say, even in the best mediumship. This would tend to express itself, also, and perhaps conflict with your ideas, so that there would be confusion—your mind and that of the medium. This complicates matters, and makes it difficult to sift the wheat from the chaff in these mediumistic communications. For, on any theory, the spiritual entity must manifest itself *through* the medium.

Other theories have been advanced by way of attempting to account for these extraordinary phenomena. One of these is telepathy or thought-transference. We know that this exists and that it seemingly occurs regardless of time and space. This being so, it may be thought: If I go to a medium, such as Mrs. Piper, and she tells me all sorts of things about my relatives, what is to prevent her from reading my mind, and getting all these facts from *it,* instead of from the spirits of the dead? Perhaps we need not invoke the spirits at all, in order to find an adequate explanation!

Of course, this is the crux of the whole problem, and there are many opinions concerning it, even among those who are convinced of the facts themselves. From the scientific standpoint, we must agree to discount all facts which are known to the sitter (even if forgotten) and assume that these *may* have been gained by thought-transference.

But many facts are told which the sitter never knew. What then? We should have to assume that the mind of the medium somehow reached out into space and contacted other living minds which *did* know them. It is extremely difficult to obtain material known to *no* living person. So that, if this sort of unlimited telepathy is accepted, it becomes increasingly difficult to prove conscious persistence.

*Mediumship and Cryptæsthesia**

It has been urged by a certain group of psychic investigators that, inasmuch as the supernormal powers of the mind seem to be almost unlimited in extent (space and time being virtually annihilated for the time being) it would be next to impossible to prove survival in consequence—no matter how strong the evidence for it might seem.

There are two replies which might be made to this objection.

(1) Such apparent omniscience is itself an extraordinary phenomenon, for which there is certainly little

---

Cryptæsthesia. A term proposed by Prof. Richet to designate knowledge gained supernormally by any means, such as telepathy, clairvoyance or in any other manner.

evidence in experimental thought-transference. This power in itself (if true) would be quite incompatible with any mechanistic scheme of mind-body connection such as that held today by practically all psychologists. It virtually grants the reality and activity of mind apart from brain; and, if that were once proved, the ground would certainly be removed from under the current psychological superstructure which is based upon the inevitable connection between the two.

(2) A further weighty objection to the doctrine consists in the fact that, in practically all such reported instances of cryptæsthesia, the supernormal perceptions of the subject have been sporadic and transitory, and anything but lasting, persistent and continuous. They are on the contrary fragmentary and disjointed.

In genuine mediumistic communications, on the other hand, we seem to obtain a more or less steady stream of supernormal knowledge, consistent within itself, and purporting to emanate from a discarnate entity, whose personality, memories and characteristics are often accurately and systematically portrayed. A unified and continuous stream of thought is presented, in short, in place of the fragmentary material generally obtained by cryptæsthesia —as evidenced both in experimental and in spontaneous cases. Flashes of intelligence are in fact replaced by a continuous stream of intelligence.

These facts certainly point away from cryptæsthesia and in the direction of the spiritistic theory, as an ultimate explanation.

The human-relationship factor in these communications is another which has been perhaps insufficiently stressed in past discussions upon the subject. In the case of G. P., for example, communicating through Mrs. Piper he recognized with the proper degree of familiarity all

THE GREATEST MENTAL MEDIUM 49

those whom he had known in life, and failed to recognize those whom he had not known, but who had been introduced as sitters in order to "trip him up." We all know our friends in different relationships, and to every one of them *we* are a different "person." When meeting them on the street, we greet them in differing ways, some formally, some enthusiastically. G. P. similarly greeted all his friends, through Mrs. Piper, just as he would have, had he met them in actual life. All this is far removed from ordinary cryptæsthesia!

Take again a case noted years ago by Dr. Hyslop. At one sitting he asked that a certain person, A., might be brought to the next sitting to communicate. Sure enough, A. turned up at the next sitting, and gave some strikingly accurate tests; but—and this is the point I wish to emphasize—he also brought along an old and dear friend of his, B., who likewise communicated. Now, the appearance of B. was totally unexpected, and practically nothing was known about him by the sitter. On the spiritistic theory, it would be the most natural thing in the world for A. to bring B. with him, to participate in the "festivities," so to say; but it would be extremely difficult to formulate a logical reason, on the theory of cryptæsthesia, why B. should appear.

It was incidents such as these which ultimately forced both Hodgson and Hyslop to accept the spiritistic theory, rather than the telepathic. And in the light of such cases one can quite see the logic of their decision!

Because of these difficulties many ingenious tests have been devised of late years in order to escape this possible alternate so far as possible. What are known as postmortem letters have been tried—letters written by someone in life and sealed up, and their contents given through a medium before they were opened. Some of these have been attempted; but even if they were more successful than they have been, it is difficult to rule out clairvoyance as an explanation. Might not the medium's mind have read the sealed letter?

Then attempts have been made to obtain *parts* of a message through various mediums by what is known as cross correspondence. A part of a message is given through one medium, and a part through another, and after several such parts have been obtained, these are all patched together, and a consistent, whole message is obtained. Many of these have been tried most successfully, and in such cases it is difficult to invoke telepathy as the explanation. It would seem, rather, that one directive mind is running the whole show, so to say, from the "other side."

Again there are psychological tests, such as those described with Mrs. Eileen Garrett (A.P.I., Bulletin 1), in which a personality stamp was obtained; and in many instances information has been secured which was in *no* living mind, such as the discovery of a lost will. All such instances point quite strongly toward the spiritistic explanation as the true one.

This is a difficult and complex subject, which has been discussed over hundreds of printed pages in minute detail; and I shall not bore the reader with technicalities any longer. Suffice it to say that, after taking all the various theories into consideration and allowing for all possible difficulties, many eminent men of science, who have familiarized themselves with the facts, have emerged convinced of survival, and stated their belief that it has been proved. Dr. Hodgson tried the telepathic hypothesis for ten years, and the spiritualistic hypothesis for ten years, and at the end of that time declared that the latter was the most sane, logical and consistent one, and the only

THE GREATEST MENTAL MEDIUM 51

one capable of explaining all the facts adequately. And Dr. Hodgson was a most level-headed and cautious man!

Mrs. Piper has played an enormous part in this modern investigation; for forty years she was the star medium of the world, and today, though long past eighty, she is still alive—though her mediumship has naturally declined with her advancing years. Her place has been more or less taken by Mrs. Osborne Leonard and other, younger mediums. But, no matter what they may do, Mrs. Piper will always be remembered as the great pioneer medium who devoted her life to the cause of scientific research and who was instrumental in convincing so many of the truth of survival.

V

LABORATORY INVESTIGATIONS IN PSYCHIC PHENOMENA

It has often been said that Aristotle possessed as fine an intellect as the world has ever seen. Yet any schoolboy today knows more of the real nature of our world than did Aristotle. Why? Because certain instruments of precision have made this exact knowledge possible. They have enabled us to *know*, where previously we have had to guess or speculate.

The same holds true in psychic science. Researches conducted within the past few years have enabled us to make great progress in this field also. For psychical research is a science like any other.

Many have asked: "How is it possible to subject the spiritual world to material investigation? How can spiritual forces be measured by physical instruments?"

It must be remembered that in cases of physical phenomena a living material body is present—that of the medium. The body and vitality of this person must constitute an intermediary of some sort between the two worlds. Suppose a phenomenon takes place. Perhaps a table is raised from the floor and floats about the room without visible means of support. Some mechanism must be employed, some unknown energy is involved which is capable of examination under precise laboratory tests. Unknown forces or energies, either within or without the medium's body, lend themselves to such investigation. Hence the need of a psychic laboratory.

LABORATORY INVESTIGATIONS

Sir William Crookes employed such methods, it will be remembered, in his famous work with the medium D. D. Home. Various scientific groups in Europe studied Eusapia Palladino in their laboratories, and within the past decades other mediums, such as Stella C., and Willi and Rudi Schneider, have been subjected to ingenious tests which would have been impossible a generation ago. They were only rendered possible because of the progress of science in other fields.

Let us consider two experiments (one earlier, one later), both devised to test the same thing—the presence of some invisible substance or energy capable of affecting matter. The first was tried in Naples about forty years ago by Professor Bottazzi and his associates.

An air-tight drum was provided, across the top of which a membrane was stretched. There was a small hole in the side of the drum, and into this was inserted a piece of strong rubber tubing. The other end of this tube was connected to what is known as a manometer. This device registers air pressure by raising a fluid on one side of a U-shaped tube, or making a bubble run along a scale. A cork float on the surface of the fluid supported an inked pen which marked a moving strip of paper revolving on a drum driven by clockwork. The point of the experiment was simply this. If some invisible entity or energy pressed upon the membrane covering the large drum, the air within it would then be forced down the rubber tube to the manometer, displacing the fluid. As the float on the surface rose and fell, its fluctuations would be graphically traced upon the strip of paper passing beneath the pen.

This apparatus was tried at several séances with Eusapia Palladino.

The second experiment of this kind was conducted by Dr. Eugène Osty of Paris, head of the Metapsychic Institute. The subject was the young medium Rudi Schneider, and the tests took place in Dr. Osty's laboratory.

It had always been noted that objects were moved in the vicinity of the medium's body; that is, within a few feet. This led to the suggestion that some subtle energy radiates from the body and affects matter in its immediate neighborhood.

What is this subtle energy and how does it operate? In order to throw light upon this question, Dr. Osty placed the objects to be moved upon a small table. Across the top of the table he passed a beam of infra-red rays. These were, of course, invisible to the eyes of those present, but the apparatus was so designed that if any solid object was interposed in the path of the rays, cutting off as much as thirty percent of them, a battery of cameras would be exposed, flashlights ignited and pictures taken of the tabletop at that moment. This would happen if any material thing tried to move the objects—say a human hand. A series of photos would at once reveal the fraud.

In the sittings which ensued, objects were moved on numerous occasions; flashes were set off, and the plates developed. What did they show? Nothing—that is, nothing abnormal. They just showed the tabletop. But *something* had nevertheless been moving about over the table because the beam of infra-red rays had been interfered with and the objects had been displaced.

Evidently some *invisible* substance or energy was at work. What was its nature? Would it be possible to find out anything about it which would be of scientific interest? That was Dr. Osty's next task.

Accordingly, he devised and put into operation another piece of apparatus by means of which it would be possible to register the oscillation or vibration rate of this invisible

LABORATORY INVESTIGATIONS 55

substance once it had begun to manifest itself by interfering with the infra-red light beam.

He had not long to wait. In the sittings which followed, the ghostly emanation began to register its presence by the movement of small objects upon the tabletop. Then it caused the second piece of apparatus (a specially built galvanometer) to record its exact pulsation. It was somewhat like taking the pulse of an invisible being standing before them in space!

And this "astral pulse beat" showed something very remarkable when its speed came to be accurately measured. For it corresponded to something actually living which could also be measured. But before we can tell just what that was, we must first of all explain something else which happened during these séances.

The ordinary breathing rate of anyone not engaged in active exercise is about 14-16 to the minute. But when Rudi Schneider goes into trance an extraordinary thing happens. His breathing rate increases to 200, 250, even 300 and more respirations per minute, and he keeps this up for considerable periods of time. This fact has naturally been of great interest to doctors, and they have studied it at considerable length. They have found that, despite its speed, this rapid breathing has no effect upon the body—itself a remarkable fact.

However, when Dr. Osty came to measure these respirations and compare them with the recorded speed of the invisible substance, he found that the vibration rate of the latter was always exactly twice that of the former! In other words, if the breathing rate was 200 to the minute, the rate of the psychic substance or energy was 400; if the medium's breathing rate went up to 250 a minute, the vibration rate of the substance measured 500 to the minute. There is evidently a most interesting connection here between the bodily activities of the medium and the psychic factors involved. We find a connection between the supernormal and physiology.

It is facts such as these which have caused a whole group of scientific men in Europe to speak of the new science of supernormal biology. We still seem to be dealing with living organisms, and hence with biology—but not with the biology known to science today! Doubtless this will constitute one of the fields for research in the future.

Interesting laboratory experiments have also been tried in other directions. For example, one of the commonest forms of ghostly manifestations, according to tradition, is the cold breeze which accompanies such visitations. We find this referred to in many ghost stories, both ancient and modern, and it is also mentioned by Job in the Old Testament.

Now it has always been thought that this sensation of cold which the subject experienced was purely subjective. It was supposed to have no external reality at all. Allegedly, the seer shivered and felt cold because he was frightened, and his story was usually disbelieved in consequence. But the reality of such cold breezes has now been definitely proved by means of self-recording thermometers—which are not frightened and not subject to hallucinations.

Doubtless you have seen such thermometers in the windows of opticians and scientific instrument-makers. They consist of a temperature scale, a revolving drum fitted with a ruled chart, and a pen which draws a line to indicate the temperature from minute to minute. In this way a graph is obtained of temperature fluctuations throughout the day.

LABORATORY INVESTIGATIONS 57

A thermometer such as this was enclosed in a cage of wire netting, and fastened to a beam on the wall by means of screws. The clockwork was set going just before the séance commenced, and of course it began registering the heat of the room.

In the séance which followed, a number of extraordinary physical phenomena were noted, among them complete liftings or levitations of the table. Coinciding with these manifestations, the thermometer showed instantaneous drops in temperature of ten, fifteen, and up to twenty degrees Fahrenheit. And these drops only took a second or two to bring about, and they coincided exactly with the psychic phenomenon taking place elsewhere in the room. Thus, science was able to measure another remarkable fact.

One more experiment of this kind was conducted by Mr. Harry Price of London, in the National Laboratory for Psychic Research. The medium used was the one who secured the extraordinary thermal changes just mentioned. Incidentally, she was not a professional medium, took no money for her services, and was not herself particularly interested in the results. She has since married and given up her mediumship entirely. The object of the experiment was to prove conclusively that a new force unknown to science was being employed under conditions that permitted no conceivable form of fraud or trickery.

The apparatus was simple and effective. Inside a flat metal bowl, mounted on a stand, was placed a regular telegraph key. This was connected by means of heavily insulated wires to a small, red electric-light bulb which was encased in a glass cover. The only normal way to complete the circuit and light the red lamp was to depress the telegraph key. When the pressure was removed the lamp went out. The top of the bowl containing the telegraph key was sealed over with a soap bubble. (By employing glycerine and castile soap in right proportions, it is possible to blow bubbles which will last for hours.) Over this was then inverted a glass cover, and then the whole piece of apparatus was placed inside a wire-netting cage and enclosed in a larger, lattice-work cage of wood. A dim light made the medium visible throughout the sitting, and she was held hand and foot, as usual, by two investigators.

During the séance the key was depressed a number of times and the lamp lighted. Examination of the apparatus, at the end of the period, showed both cages intact, the glass bowl in place, *and the soap bubble unbroken!* This was one of the most conclusive tests of this kind ever undertaken.

These are but a few of the many hundreds of experiments made during the past few years in which instruments of precision have been used to check the results. But even from these it can be seen that important laboratory work is now being undertaken in this field and that great progress is being made in the purely scientific aspects of such phenomena. More and more, the latest discoveries are being applied, and infra-red photography, moving pictures, special cameras and lenses, various specially built devices such as magnetometers and biometers, are being employed in scientific investigations.

It is apparent that in the field of *physical* phenomena there are endless tests which might be undertaken. But good, reliable physical mediums are rare—especially those willing to lend themselves to scientific scrutiny. So it becomes a question of "first catch your hare!" In the absence of such mediums, one might well ask whether certain types of mental mediums might not lend themselves to laboratory investigation also. Fortunately, the answer is yes.

LABORATORY INVESTIGATIONS

At first sight, it might appear impossible to subject mental mediums to tests of this character. How enclose a stream of thought in a test tube? Of course, that can't be done, but it is possible to do something almost as good, as was proved when the American Psychical Institute began its experiments with an English medium, Mrs. Eileen Garrett, well known on both sides of the Atlantic.

Mrs. Garrett is one of those rare mediums who will subject herself to any sort of scientific investigation, and has been tested by leading universities and scientific groups in Europe and America. She herself is frankly "on the fence" with regard to the phenomena she is instrumental in producing; she wants to find out about them and to discover whether they are what they claim to be or not. Hence her willing cooperation.

The most striking of Mrs. Garrett's phenomena occur when she is in a deep trance. She merely sits in a large, comfortable chair, and seemingly goes to sleep. A few minutes later, however, she leans forward, crosses her arms across her breast, and begins talking. The intelligence that manifests itself claims to be that of a native of Asia Minor who lived about a hundred years ago. His name is Uvani, and he is Mrs. Garrett's regular control.

All mediums have so-called controls of this sort, whose duty it is to relay messages and get in touch with other spiritual beings not of this world. Mrs. Garrett also has a secondary control, less frequently in evidence, named Abdul Latif, who is called upon whenever medical diagnosis is necessary.

Who or what is this control-personality, Uvani? Is he, in truth, a spiritual entity, as he claims to be? Is he merely a part of the medium's subconscious mind, play-acting the part—as nearly all psychologists would contend? Is he some "X" of a nature still unknown? This is a very important question to settle, since it bears upon the whole problem of survival. It was in an attempt to solve this question, or at least to throw light upon it, that a long series of experimental sittings was held with Mrs. Garrett in which instrumental checks were used.

In order that the reader may fully understand the nature of these tests and their significance, one or two preliminary explanations are necessary. Each person in the world is different from every other person; that is what makes us all different, one from another. These differences are due to our past lives, our experiences, environment, memories, associations, and dozens of other factors. In the course of our lives we have all had varied experiences—some pleasant, some unpleasant. Associated with these past memories are emotions of greater or lesser intensity. Whenever a past experience is recalled, the emotions connected with it are also aroused, although the subject may be quite unaware of this.

Some may have had unpleasant experiences connected with water, others with mountains, others with cats, others with snakes, and so on. Others may have had happy or unhappy memories in connection with an entirely different set of things. So that, if we were to take a long list of words and read them off to a number of individuals in turn, we should find that they differed in their reactions one from another. The response of no two would be exactly alike, either in the emotions aroused by the words or in the intensity of the emotions themselves.

Word-lists of such a nature have been compiled and have been used by psychoanalysts in treating their patients. One of the standard lists was prepared by Dr. C. G. Jung of Zürich, and that was the list we used in testing Mrs. Garrett.

A list of 100 words is read to the subject, one word at a time, and he is instructed to reply to each word by some other word which pops into his head at once. He must not stop to think or control the reply he makes. His response should be made instantaneously. For example:

Stimulus Word	Response Word
Lamp	Light
Blood	Red
Water	Swim
Stem	Leaf

The responses represent the memory associations in the subject's mind.

The length of time the subject takes in replying is known as the reaction time and this is measured by means of a stop watch, in tenths of a second. If an unusually long time is taken in responding to any particular word, the analyst knows that there is a certain subconscious resistance to that word causing a blockage or an unpleasant emotional association that has been recalled by the stimulus word. In this way the emotions which have been bothering the subject are unearthed, and when they have been eradicated, the patient is theoretically cured.

So, in testing any subject, we have one, the response words, and two, the reaction times. These taken together constitute a sort of personality-stamp, or psychic thumb-print, so to speak. Theoretically, this would be just as true of the dead as of the living, since every person is supposed to retain his personality, memories, and associations in after-life. The individual thoughts and emotions should be the same in both cases.

We come to the third and last part of this test. It is a well-known fact that, if a weak electric current is passed through the human body, its flow can be measured by means of a delicate device known as a galvanometer. The greater the emotion aroused, the more current passes through the body, and the greater the swing of the needle as shown by the number of divisions on the scale. This instrument has been extensively used in the law courts and is popularly known as the lie detector. Its chief value lies in the fact that it is fraud-proof. No matter how hard he may try, the subject cannot influence the results materially. If a word or a question arouses an emotion within him, then the instrument shows it, the galvanometer needle swings over and the variation is recorded. Hardened criminals have been detected by it.

We are now ready to assemble all these complicated facts and show you how they work when testing a medium by such instrumental means. The medium takes her seat in a comfortable chair, and copper wires are attached to her hands by means of electrodes, connecting her with the galvanometer. The prepared word-list is then read to her slowly, one word at a time, and her responses noted by the observer. The length of time she takes in replying to each individual word is likewise recorded. We have here, therefore, a triple check: reaction words, reaction times, and galvanometer deflections.

The medium now passes into trance, and her conscious mind departs and is replaced by that of her control. The word-list is then read to the control, as it had previously been read to the medium, and in turn his reaction words, reaction times, and galvanometer deflections are noted. By doing this over and over again, a mass of figures and words are obtained which are capable of statistical comparison and an analysis to determine how much they resemble or differ from each other. If the results are similar we know that we are dealing with the same mind, or some part of it, while if they prove to be very different, it would seem to indicate that two separate and distinct minds—that of the medium and that of the control—have been tested.

LABORATORY INVESTIGATIONS

In our experiments with Mrs. Garrett we obtained very remarkable differences between the control-personality and the medium herself. Even more striking, however, was the sequel to all this. We asked her control, Uvani, whether it would be possible for him to find a number of other persons and induce *them* to reply to these lists of words. Uvani said that he thought this was possible; he would try!

We had, in all, seven different entities who communicated in this way, and when their responses were compared, it was found that they all differed from the medium, and all differed from her control in emotional tone, in time-reactions and in the character of the words chosen for replying to the word-lists. So we *seemed* to be dealing with seven different minds, rather than with one, as shown by the instrumental and psychological tests! How valid are these results?

More recent investigations have shown that the galvanometer and time-reactions may not in fact be as conclusive as they were originally thought to be; however the word-reactions—that is, the characteristic responses we obtained from the seemingly different entities—still remain highly significant and important, and are at least indicative of the operation of different minds. This is a long and controversial subject, into which we have not the space to enter now. The above will at least serve to illustrate the point, that laboratory methods may be applied even in the investigation of mental mediumship, while they are absolutely indispensable when studying physical phenomena. Here they have proved of the utmost value. The interested reader will find this subject thoroughly covered in my book *Laboratory Investigations into Psychic Phenomena,* to which he is referred for further details concerning this fascinating subject.

VI

TRUMPET MEDIUMS

TRUMPET MEDIUMS, so-called, are those in whose presence independent voices are produced—almost invariably in the dark—theoretically separate and apart from the vocal apparatus of the medium. Usually horns or trumpets are employed, through which these voices come and into which they speak. They serve to magnify and direct the sounds or voices produced, which often carry on long conversations with the sitters. They are moved about in the air, during the séance, for that purpose.

My own experience with mediums of this type has been most unsatisfactory. Though I have sat with many of them through a period of years, every one of them upon investigation proved to be palpably fraudulent. (In every case the medium simply lifted the trumpet in the dark and talked into it, imitating the various voices heard.) There are three possible exceptions to this sweeping denunciation—all more or less dubious. The first was a single incident in the "Margery case," when a series of whistles and whisperings were heard in the corner of the room, while every mouth was theoretically covered by the hand of his neighbor.* The second was the case of Thomas Lacey, of Toronto; and the third was the case of William Cartheuser, of Los Angeles. I propose to discuss these cases in some detail.

Let us take first the case of Thomas Lacey. In 1936-37

---

*I had more than fifty sittings with the celebrated "Margery," as a member of the "Scientific American" Committee, in 1924.

TRUMPET MEDIUMS

my wife and I had a series of sittings with this medium, at the request of the White Brotherhood, of Canada, some of whose members had sat with Lacey for several years. Some preliminary sittings were held in New York, and we afterwards visited Toronto, where several sittings were held in the Grotto, an underground chamber, hewn out of the solid rock, which had been built by the White Brotherhood. Two sittings were also held in the local radio station, in order that certain instrumental checks might be tried, as to the degree of independence of the voice.

For this purpose, three microphones were installed in the séance room: one directly in front of the medium, one about eight feet to the left, and the third approximately the same distance to the right—both about five feet in front of him. The three microphones thus constituted a sort of triangle, at one corner of which the medium was seated.

The object of this test was to see whether one of the seemingly independent voices might not speak more clearly and with greater volume into one of the more distant microphones than into the one nearest the medium —which difference in volume and tonal quality might be picked up in the recording room of the radio station. On theory, if a voice were recorded as being louder and clearer in either of the two distant microphones than in the one nearest the medium (while the medium was still seated in his chair) this would indicate the proximity of the voice to that microphone, and hence, seemingly, a certain degree of independence of the voice from the physical organism of the medium.

Unfortunately, owing mainly to the imperfection of the technique employed, it was found impossible to decide this question with any degree of accuracy. Three separate leads should have been provided instead of only one, allowing adequate comparisons to be made at the same time. Various attempts were seemingly made by one of the controls to approach one of these distant microphones, but the inadequate evidence available seemed to indicate that the voice at all times originated from a point in space in the immediate vicinity of the medium's body, and hence by inference emanated from his throat.

Despite the relatively inconclusive nature of these preliminary tests, it was nevertheless felt that more evidence was available for seeming independence than was shown by the instruments employed, and that a *prima facie* case was established for further research along these lines. The unrecorded and unofficial evidence for this apparent independence was at times quite impressive. Unfortunately, the limited time at our disposal, plus the difficulty of obtaining the further cooperation of the radio station, rendered such additional instrumental tests impossible.

As to the actual content of the messages received through Lacey's mediumship, really evidential material was almost entirely lacking. This was perhaps largely due to the fact that the members of the White Brotherhood were not particularly interested in this aspect of his phenomena, but rather in the philosophical material they received. Lacey's band of controls comprised an amazing assortment of eminent personalities, including King George, W. T. Stead, Lawrence of Arabia, Edison, and heaven knows who else, in addition to his regular controls, "The White Brother," and "Violet." Some of the impersonations were quaintly impressive; but one could hardly take them very seriously. We did however attempt various psychological tests of these various personalities, and received characteristically different replies to the questions asked.

For example, we requested all of them to give, in turn, their answers to the four following questions, selected from the Thurston Attitude Scale. They were:

1. What is your opinion of the theory of evolution?
2. What is your opinion as to the treatment of criminals?
3. What is your attitude toward birth control?
4. What is your attitude in regard to Sunday observance?

All our alleged communicators replied to these questions quite differently, as might be expected, and many of their replies were in keeping with the personality supposedly communicating at the time. However, they might well have been the *sort* of replies which the medium imagined they *would* give; so that we could not, as I say, take them too seriously.

More striking, in a way, were the replies which the medium himself gave (in a normal state) when attached to a galvanometer (lie detector). A number of pointed questions were asked him regarding the authenticity of his own phenomena—whether he considered them genuine, and so on. On theory, he might well have replied in the affirmative, while the instrument would indicate that he was not telling the truth. (This test was of course analogous to that tried in the case of Mrs. Garrett.) On the whole, it must be admitted that Lacey emerged from this ordeal quite well, the device seeming to show that he was telling the truth. Difficulties and blockages were noted, it is true, but none of these was really condemnatory. The fundamental sincerity of the medium, therefore, seemed to be borne out by these tests.

Our tentative conclusion was that Lacey was instrumental in producing enough sufficiently interesting phenomena, both physical and mental, to make his case worthy of further investigation. This in itself is something—for a trumpet medium!

We come, now, to our third and most interesting case —that of William Cartheuser. Here we have a far more difficult and complicated problem on our hands. I cannot do better, perhaps, than present this case in the form of a preliminary report which was written immediately after our series of sittings with him, during which a number of interesting instrumental tests were tried. Our report runs in part as follows:

William Cartheuser is a trumpet medium, instrumental in obtaining so-called independent voices. These are said to be produced independently of the vocal apparatus of the medium, and carry on conversations with the sitters.

These sittings are all held in total darkness, and the medium usually is not held or directly controlled in any way. Occasionally some sort of control is, however, permitted, details of which will be given in due course.

The medium himself is undersized, and gives the impression of being reticent, introverted, apprehensive and constantly on the defensive. His eyes are light blue and of a peculiar quality. He has a hare-lip and cleft palate, which cause a severe impediment in his speech. A photograph of himself, taken when he was about six years of age, shows this hare-lip very plainly. This impediment, however, seems to affect only certain words (the labials particularly), and part of his conversation is relatively clear and intelligible. This is of interest in view of the clarity of the séance-voices, most of which seem to be clear, though subdued or whispered for the most part.

Cartheuser is of German extraction, and lived for some years in Europe as a child. He states that he went to school in Transylvania. This may account for the smattering of foreign languages which he occasionally displays; though it would *not* account for ready to-and-fro conversations in Polish, Russian, etc., *if* verified.

The quality, timbre and loudness of the voices coming through the trumpet varies greatly. Once or twice, during any given sitting, there may be a loud shout, or guttural laugh, but this is instantaneous and never sustained. One or two conversations have been carried on in a fairly normal voice; but the majority of them are low and indistinct, or whispered, so that they have been hard to catch and record, unless the microphone is directly in front of the trumpet employed.

The enunciation of the voices, however, even if weak, has usually been fairly clear and understandable. There are some variations in these voices, though one cannot avoid the impression that Cartheuser-characteristics lie behind most of them. The female voices, especially—such as that of the alleged control Elsie—seem to be obviously a male voice disguised as a falsetto.

Many of these voices, even when purporting to come from a communicating spirit, obviously display the desires and wishes of the medium himself. His comments on certain sitters, the conditions involved, his avid desire for money, his native tendency to scandal and what may be termed "bathroom stories," all are manifested in his alleged communications. On the other hand references are occasionally made to names and events which the medium could not (apparently) have known. This indicates definitely supernormal phenomena. We shall come to these statements a little later on.

Another obvious peculiarity is the grammar employed in these communications. Normally the medium is fairly well spoken, though he employs simple language with which to express his thoughts. Occasionally, however, he lapses into bad grammar, and it was noticeable that, on several occasions, the séance-voice has similarly lapsed—to the extent that it has been commented upon and corrected by the sitters.

Of course spiritualists have an explanation for this. Their claim is that, inasmuch as the communicating entity must necessarily *utilize* the physical organism of the medium (in this case the speaking apparatus) it must perforce take on some of the tricks and peculiarities of that organism—involuntary habits and movements, expressions and tricks of speech, and so on. Thus, the physical and mental mechanism of the medium must necessarily color and influence the character of the communications, to some extent. This explanation may be a perfectly valid one, so far as it goes. It becomes unacceptable, however, when applied to statements quite contrary to known beliefs and memories of the alleged communicator, representing errors in fact, or viewpoints diametrically opposed to those formerly held by the assumed entity. For example, one can quite understand the possibility of difficulties involved in speaking Polish through a medium who knows *no* Polish; but *not* fluent conversation in English when the deceased person knew not a word of English in life! Incidents such as these tell strongly against the spiritualistic theory—at least as commonly held.

Coupled with this are the numerous cases in which the medium has obviously resorted to guessing, fishing and innuendo, in order to obtain information, as well as frank inquiry regarding sitters! Thus, after the first sitting, Cartheuser frequently asked us by 'phone who was going to be present that evening, and what we knew regarding them. Evidently feeling the desirability of impressing one member of the circle, for example, after discovering that he had seen and talked with the President several times, he asked us quite frankly whether he was a Senator, whether he lived in Washington, what his business was, whether or not he could be considered a financial magnate, etc. Such questioning (often leaving us half amused and half astounded at his effrontery in asking such data from researchers) naturally did not lead to favorable impressions.

On the other hand, and as opposed to this, is the fact that Cartheuser seems in many ways to be simple, naive and sincere. One gains the impression that he is a curious mixture of naivete and cunning. Certainly the man's personality undergoes an interesting transformation during a séance. He becomes more positive, more assured, more mentally agile. The quips and responses often seem to be more shrewd and spontaneous than he would be capable of in normal life. One gains the impression that his usual personality has been, to some extent at least, overshadowed by some other personality, more alert than his own. Assuming that some slight dissociation takes place, during the séance (as he claims) an analogy might perhaps be drawn between Cartheuser and that of Eddie Bergen, who in real life (according to reports) is shy, reticent and bashful; but with Charlie McCarthy on his knee, indulges in bold quips, risqué stories and almost impertinent observations. The ventriloquist's personality has undergone a change, in short, characteristic of the impersonation. Perhaps something of the sort occurs in the case of Cartheuser.

During the séance Cartheuser claims to be under the guidance of certain alleged spirit controls—"Elsie," "Dr. Anderson," and others. There is, we think, thus far no evidence whatever of the existence and independence of these so-called controls. None of them has, to our knowledge, ever attempted to establish his or her identity by supplying verifiable data as to their earth lives. On the contrary, Dr. Anderson claimed to have lectured in Chicago "a hundred and fifty years ago," when there was *no* Chicago at that time! Elsie is supposed to be a fully matured woman of about thirty-two years of age; she nevertheless speaks in a childish voice (obviously falsetto) which indicates an intelligence of about eight or nine. In this case it cannot even be claimed that this is for purposes of identification—since none of the sitters knew her in life. They all seemingly represent conscious or subconscious concoctions on the part of the medium.

From one point of view it is immaterial *what* they are, since there are many cases on record in which these alleged controls have obviously been of this same character, and yet, whatever they are, they have apparently succeeded in bringing through other communicators who *did* identify themselves, or who succeeded in supplying valuable supernormal information. Even assuming them to be subconscious fabrications, therefore, would not necessarily negate their utility, since, whatever they are, they constitute an invaluable connecting link, without whose presence the medium could not adequately function. We seem driven to accept them, therefore, no matter what their ultimate nature may prove to be.

Irrespective of these controls, other personalities claimed to communicate during the series of sittings held with Cartheuser. Without knowing these personalities in life, just estimates by outsiders are obviously hard to form, but we gained the impression—subject to the above proviso—that these communications were anything but characteristic; in short, that there was but the scantiest evidence of their being actually present and communicating at the time. The spiritualistic interpretation of these messages therefore seemed to us most doubtful. The recipients of these messages are in many respects in a far better position than ourselves to arrive at a just estimate of their verisimilitude; but our own opinion is that no real evidence was furnished, at any time, of their active and conscious participation.

All this is not saying that Cartheuser does not, at times, apparently obtain supernormal information, or make successful "hits." Some of the material given seems strongly to indicate this. Isolated names and references indicate their telepathic origin. Others are even more difficult to account for. These facts in themselves justify one's interest in his case, showing that we have here an interesting psychological problem. On any theory he is a case well worth studying.

If Cartheuser went into trance, during his sittings, some of the problems arising from them would be to some extent simplified; but he remains apparently normal throughout, and is at least mentally alert to the extent that he knows (often to an uncanny degree) what the sitters are thinking and doing, and knows everything that the voices are saying, and so forth. He can always understand and repeat these remarks. It is quite possible, however, that a certain mental dissociation does occur during the séances, perhaps quite unknown to him, and that the sly, shrewd and tricky self which is then manifested is different from his own normal personality—just as, in many cases of multiple personality, the secondary self displays characteristics completely at variance with the normal self. In his normal life, Cartheuser gives the impression of being a simple, sincere and straightforward little fellow. If some such psychological transformation as that suggested takes place during his séances, this would perhaps account in some degree for the characteristics above described.

There are brief flashes during his sittings when seemingly characteristic messages and intonations of voice express themselves and, though these seem to be relatively fleeting and evanescent, they are nevertheless to that extent impressive.

Regarding the supernormal knowledge actually displayed in our sittings, none of this seemingly equals much that had formerly been obtained, for example, in some of the sittings attended by Dawn Edwards in California. However, a number of such accurate "hits" were given, some of which might have resulted from clever inferences from what had gone before, but some of which were seemingly "out of the blue," and impressive for that reason. As examples of the former, much of the material given Mr. X., one of the sitters, seems to us to be obviously inferential. He is a man of deep sentiment and spiritual nature (as disclosed by his previous open discussion of religion), and as such might well carry with him a little book, in which there might well be a photograph, and perhaps some crushed flowers. On the other hand, many names were given which remained totally unrecognized, while numerous erroneous statements were made.

Opposed to this, information was seemingly given on some occasions, which the medium could not possibly have known, and which he would be most unlikely to guess. Thus, at one sitting, several most unusual names were given quite correctly. It is interesting to remark, however, that the follow-up material on all these names was totally wrong. In other words, Cartheuser seemed to get occasional genuine flashes of information, which further conscious or subconscious elaboration on his part very largely discounted and destroyed. The mere fact that he does occasionally get these flashes, however, makes his case one worth continued and systematic investigation.

Summing up his mental phenomena, therefore, one may conclude that, while there is scant evidence of communication, there is good ground for suspecting, at least on some occasions, that Cartheuser actually obtained supernormal information which was given through the trumpet. This more or less agrees with the conclusions of Henry C. McComas, Professor of Psychology, Johns Hopkins University, based on his sittings with Cartheuser. (*Ghosts I Have Talked With*, p. 52.)

Trumpet and Other Physical Phenomena

Coming now to his physical manifestations, we are certainly on far more debatable ground. Great complications and difficulties presented themselves—due largely to the fact that no holding or rigid control was permitted throughout the sittings, and, by agreement, no tests were undertaken without his knowledge and sanction. This agreement we rigidly adhered to. It involved not only no "grabbings," and sudden flashing of lights, but no photographs taken without his cue, no tests such as the electrically-connected chair. Inasmuch as the sittings were held in pitch darkness, visual observations were excluded, and one had to rely on hearing, backed up by such scant tactile and visual observations as one could make.

Three trumpets in all were employed during our sittings—two provided by Cartheuser and one by ourselves. Our trumpet was painted with a band of luminous paint at *both* ends—to enable one to locate the mouth or small end of the trumpet in the dark, and ascertain whether or not it was in the proximity of the medium's mouth. Unfortunately, this trumpet was not used during the sittings, being thrown out of the circle on every occasion soon after the séance started. This being the case we ceased to place our trumpet in the circle after the third sitting, using only the two of the medium's. These, however, were ordinary tin trumpets, free from any preparation, and were inspected on several occasions. They are the ordinary trumpets sold for the purpose.

One of these trumpets, painted with a luminous band at the large or far end, is in three sections; the other, with *no* luminous band, is in four. It is interesting to note that, while the shorter trumpet was always opened at the beginning of the séance, the longer one was always placed on the floor collapsed, and at the conclusion of the séance was found collapsed—never open. One cannot help feeling that there was a definite purpose in this—to prevent the sitters from noting the great extensile reach of the longer trumpet when fully opened. Thinking only in terms of the shorter trumpet, it would not be realized that the reach of the longer one was fully a foot further—giving, with the medium's arm, a considerable range. Another point of interest is the fact that the medium gathers his trumpets together immediately after the sitting, and packs them in his case. If one or both trumpets were wet from the moisture of the breath, this would be quite understandable; but there would seem to be no valid excuse for this great haste otherwise.

The movements of the trumpets were either very fast or very slow. Occasionally they would swish through the air with great speed, sometimes seemingly in puzzling circular orbits. On the other hand, touches were made when the trumpet was moving very slowly, especially on the far side of the circle. These touches were often made on request, and with great accuracy. It is difficult to see how many of these could have been made unless the

TRUMPET MEDIUMS

medium had the ability to see in the dark. Science does not recognize this ability. Even the eyes of a cat have to have *some* light in order to see; and in pitch blackness the cat cannot see either. Yet someone or something seemingly had the faculty of seeing very well in the dark, and the trumpet would often touch a sitter, seated at a considerable distance from the medium, without hesitation or fumbling. This to us was one of the most interesting and baffling phenomena in connection with Cartheuser's sittings, and seems to us to warrant prolonged investigation and study.

Touches made by the trumpets in the immediate vicinity of the medium present no very great difficulty. On a number of occasions, however, persons sitting eight or nine feet from the medium were touched, when we felt certain that the medium was in his chair. On the theory of fraud only two logical explanations present themselves. Either Cartheuser attached the trumpet to some reaching rod device (he was never searched), or he might have inserted the small end of one trumpet into the end of the other, so as to give him the length of *both* trumpets (minus the ten inches or so used for this insertion). In either case we should expect to find the further trumpet moved about with great care and relatively slowly—which is precisely what we did find. There were two or three instances, however, where this explanation seems hardly sufficient, notably a series of touches on Mr. Silverberg's hand and arm with considerable *rapidity;* and, as he pointed out when discussing the phenomenon after the sitting was over, it would be most difficult if not impossible to produce a series of *rapid* touches when the distance and leverage was so great. We must be content, therefore, to leave some of these touches for the moment unexplained.

Coming to the physical characteristics of the voices heard through the trumpets, most of them were subdued or whispered, though we occasionally got loud yells and laughs. The sound of breathing was, however, clearly audible throughout the conversations, showing that breath was necessary and that some breathing mechanism was employed. This being so, it was decided to obtain, if possible, a chemical test of the nature of this breath. A bottle of lime water was accordingly provided, into the mouth of which was inserted a glass tube. The spirit was requested to blow down this tube, so as to make the lime water bubble. Normally, the carbonic acid gas exhaled from the human lungs will cause a cloudy precipitate in the lime water, indicating its presence. When tried, however, the "spirit" blew into the tube for only a very few seconds (too short a time to get a definite reaction) and the bottle was then knocked over, spilling the greater part of its contents. We had hoped to repeat this test on other occasions, but no further opportunity to do so presented itself during the last sittings.

Two naturalistic explanations of these voices may be mentioned—only to be dismissed. These are (a) hallucination, and (b) ventriloquism. Regarding the former, everyone in the circle heard the voices simultaneously, though not always with the same distinctness, which would be quite natural, under the circumstances. Furthermore, records of the voices were taken, and a series of phonograph records amply dispose of the hallucination theory!

As to the latter: every professional ventriloquist agrees that it is impossible to produce true ventriloquial effects *in the dark;* distraction of attention is necessary, plus vocal effects. We have discussed this question at considerable length, however, elsewhere. (*The Story of Psychic Science,* pp. 154-56; *Journal A.S.P.R.,* August, 1926.)

One question of great interest comes up in connection with Cartheuser's voices, and that is the possibility of their *overlapping*—of two or more spirit voices talking at the same time, or a voice talking while the medium is talking (normally). We have heard many such accounts in the past, not only in connection with Cartheuser's sittings, but of other mediums as well. Putting aside the present series of sittings, for the moment, we may say that our own experience with trumpet mediums in the past has been entirely negative. On no occasion have we ever been enabled to detect such duplication or simultaneity—though others at the séance declared they heard it. Always there has been a rapid shifting back and forth of the two voices, sometimes so rapidly that one would almost be willing to swear that they were absolutely simultaneous. Careful attention however disclosed the fact that they were *not*. This is merely our own experience, which is quite at variance with the testimony of other investigators, who have declared that they have heard two or three voices talking or singing at the same time. (*Cf.,* for example, Vice-Admiral Moore's book *The Voices.*) Judgment on this point must therefore be held in suspense.

In Cartheuser's sittings, duplication of voices often *seemed* to occur, whereas, as a matter of fact, only rapid alternation was resorted to. On the other hand, there were two or three instances where such absolute simultaneity seemed to be evidenced. In one case, in particular, one of us (H. C.) was sitting quite close to the medium, and listening most attentively to the whispered conversation which was going on through the trumpet, while a grunting voice said several words to Mr. Silverberg, seated near the recording apparatus, some nine feet away. This brief overlapping of the two voices seemed absolutely certain, on that occasion, and was noted with great care at the time. It was a most baffling phenomenon!

If this observation is correct, it renders possible the duplication of voices on other occasions when it was less clearly noted. Certainly one gained the impression during the sittings that it occurred fairly frequently!

In order to check this possibility more accurately, several additional tests were undertaken. *Two* microphones were provided, one to record the medium's normal voice when speaking, the other to detect that of the spirit. Or, if two spirits spoke at the same time, both of them could utilize a separate microphone, and the merging or intermingling of the voices would be recorded on the phonograph record. Unfortunately, this test proved abortive in that no clear-cut instances were recorded, at least during the sittings at which it was tried. Despite repeated requests, no such instance was noted. This test was introduced only relatively late in the series, however, and it is possible that, had it been tried before, such positive evidence might have been obtained. We had hoped that the phonograph records would decide this question, but, as we have said, they did not do so conclusively.

Another point of considerable interest and importance in connection with Cartheuser's voice phenomena is this: despite the fact that his normal speech is greatly affected by his hare-lip, the voices coming through the trumpet seem to be relatively clear-cut and devoid of any such defect. In order to test this further, if possible, the following test was devised. Inasmuch as labials proved the obvious stumbling block in his speech, the following word-combinations were prepared:

> Peter Piper picked a peck of pickled peppers.
> Modern man makes marvelous machines.
> Begin baking beans before breakfast.

We had planned to get a record (on the machine) of these sentences, as spoken by Cartheuser normally, asking one of the spirits to repeat them in the sitting. However, Cartheuser absolutely refused to try the experiment, or to have a record of his normal voice taken at all. This interesting test had therefore to be abandoned.

Another test which might be applied is to place a stethoscope on the throat of the medium, rendering clearly audible even the faintest articulation. Professor McComus tried this, and heard guttural sounds corresponding to the voices produced; then suddenly all voices ceased! He assumed that the medium was pinching the tube. Cartheuser has never allowed anyone to try this test since.

In addition to the touches by the trumpet, sitters are often touched by hands which have every appearance of being human hands. These touches are sometimes light, but sometimes powerful. They have pulled hair, pushed and pulled chairs, grasped sitters by their coats, and on one occasion removed the shoe of one of the sitters, on the opposite side of the circle. The hands have picked up coins, handled luminous plates and played a few chords on a violin, handling the bow in a seemingly experienced manner. In short they behave in every respect like living, human hands. Lacking evidence to the contrary, we must of course assume that these are the medium's hands; and there is evidence that in many cases they are. Our only difficulty lies in those cases which are apparently beyond his reach; but these cases are few and far between, and in many respects the touches experienced seem to us to be among the least conclusive of his phenomena.

It is to be noted, in this connection, that Cartheuser objects to continuous hand control throughout the sittings, though he occasionally permitted it during short periods.

He similarly resents tying in any form, having an aversion to any kind of natural or artificial restraint. On two occasions, when he was tied with black silk thread, no distant phenomena were noted until the threads were broken. (It should be noted here that many physical mediums have submitted to absolute rigid control throughout the sitting.)

Phonograph records were taken throughout the series, of to-and-fro conversations, and these are available for study.

Infra-red photographs were taken on several occasions, but only on the ready signal from the medium. These proved disappointing, in that no genuinely supernormal phenomenon was ever photographed. It must be admitted, however, that the fault for this lies with us to a great extent, and was due to faulty technique. The infra-red plates obtained were not those best suited for flashlight photography, and considerable experimentation was needed with bulbs, filters, and so on, before the best results were obtained. Due to the great difficulty in obtaining infra-red plates and bulbs (due to war restrictions), we were loath to expend these lavishly in prior experimentation. On one occasion, when the levitation of the trumpet was to be photographed, the flashlight failed to work properly—though it was a new one bought that day. The two photographs which were taken showed nothing abnormal upon them.

Cold breezes which had every appearance of being real and objective were often felt by the sitters in Cartheuser's séances. A self-recording minimum thermometer placed in the circle, however, failed to register any drop in temperature. These cold breezes are either subjective, therefore, or are of a character incapable of affecting an ordinary thermometer.

TRUMPET MEDIUMS

During one entire sitting the medium's occupancy of his chair was tested by means of an electric circuit. Sharp steel points were attached to the legs of the chair, these penetrating the carpet and making contact with metal plates beneath it. These plates were connected with a current, a small transformer and a tiny green light. When the medium sat in his chair, the weight of his body forced the points through the carpet onto the metal plates, completing the circuit. The lamp then remained lighted. When however the medium got up out of his chair, the resiliency of the carpet lifted the chair sufficiently to break the contact, and the light went out. Theoretically, this was a perfect method of attesting the medium's continued presence in his chair.

The initial test of this apparatus, however, showed that, as originally set up, it was inconclusive. Only two metal plates were employed, placed under pins in the rear legs; and it was shown that, by leaning forward, the contact was broken and the light extinguished, though the medium was still sitting in his chair. At the next sitting, therefore, four plates were used, and all four legs of the chair provided with pins. The result was that perfect contact was maintained, no matter how he shifted his weight in the chair, and the light was only extinguished when he got up out of it altogether. During the sitting in which this test was employed, the observer (of the green light) reported that it had remained lighted steadily throughout—that is, that the medium had never been out of his chair. Touches and other phenomena occurred nevertheless at considerable distances from the medium on this occasion.

On several occasions small lights were seen, moving about the circle at distances varying from two to six feet from the medium. These were usually described as yellow or greenish in color. They might perhaps have been produced by a small, shaded, pocket flashlight—though we naturally have no proof that they *were* so produced. Here again a prior search of the medium would have proved most valuable!

At most sittings two luminous plates were provided, that is to say metal plates, one side of which had been coated with luminous paint protected by lacquer. These were activated just before the sitting and placed, luminous side down, on the carpet. During the séance, one or both of these plates would be lifted, turned over, wafted about the circle and eventually thrown out of it with great force. On several such occasions dark fingers could be seen gripping the edges of the plates. On some occasions these fingers seemed to resemble the fingers of the medium, and at other times they did not, being apparently thinner and more delicate. Figures which had been cut out of black paper were also held against the luminous plate, so that they could be seen. On two or three occasions these were the figures asked for. (It should be noted, however, that the contour of the paper figures could be felt in the dark, by running the fingers over them.)

The box containing these paper figures also contained a number of small cardboard squares, on which were printed the letters of the alphabet. Inasmuch as these squares were all alike, it would be impossible to distinguish one from another by the sense of touch; direct vision would be necessary. We had planned asking one of the communicating entities to pick out certain letters and arrange them on the floor in the dark, spelling out, let us say, the word l-o-v-e. This test was not undertaken, however, on the two occasions when it was suggested.

A bowl of fresh flowers was always placed in the center of the circle, and on several occasions these flowers were

TRUMPET MEDIUMS

removed and deposited either in the laps of the sitters, or thrown at them, together with drops of water. These manifestations could hardly be considered impressive, however, since they depended entirely upon the ability of the medium to reach them, and they were not sufficiently far away to render this impossible.

In several of the séances a box of modeling clay was placed in the center of the circle, on the floor, and the suggestion was made that one of the spirits might leave his thumb print on the clay. In order to check possible results, fingerprints were taken of every person attending the sitting, including the medium. Faint prints were obtained, but these unfortunately proved valueless, for two reasons: (1) They were too faint for identification, and (2) several people had handled the clay, when examining it after the séance, so that the test was invalidated. We did on one occasion, however, obtain a curious impression which looked as though it might have been made by some circular metal object. At the time we could find nothing to account for this. The following weekend, however, we took Cartheuser to visit some friends of ours in Yonkers (they had asked him out to dinner and a social evening). At the dinner table Cartheuser took from his pocket a medal which had been given him by some admirers in Canada, and on handling the disk it at once became obvious to us that the impression on the clay was identical with a portion of the medal in question. The marks on the clay had evidently been produced by this medal, that is, which had been promptly returned to the medium's pocket.

We had prepared a special test in the form of a powder which, sprinkled on the surface of any object, remained totally invisible, and, even if transferred to the hand in picking up the object, it would still remain invisible *until examined in ultra-violet light.* An ultra-violet bulb was obtained for this purpose. This test has remained untried, however, because of our agreement with Cartheuser not to trick him in any way, or conduct any experiments the character of which was unknown to him. Working under less restricted conditions, we cannot but feel that this would constitute a highly effective and conclusive test.

Two tests were conducted at the eighth sitting which had not been tried before. These were (1) a netting cage, and (2) the presence of a certain amount of red light.

The cage was constructed of mosquito netting, and was about five feet square. Top, bottom and three sides were solid netting. The fourth side was left open. This side faced the couch—that is, the side *opposite* the medium. One of us (H. C.) sat on the couch, opposite the opening. The other sitters sat at the sides. The trumpets, plates and flowers were placed inside the netting cage, so that the medium could not touch them. Cartheuser himself was subjected to no other control.

We sat for an hour and fifty minutes under these conditions, but nothing whatever happened, except the falling over of the two trumpets—which might have been done by pulling the netting sharply and upsetting them. No voices and no other phenomena occurred, except a few touches on the nearest sitters. We finally gave this up and sat for another hour and a half in dim red light with the trumpets outside the cage, but again nothing happened. At the end of that time we concluded the séance.

It cannot be contended that the interposition of the netting introduced impossible conditions, because, in sittings held abroad, this test was successfully employed. Rudi Schneider succeeded in moving objects placed behind a net, and Dr. von Schrenck-Notzing published photographs of the penetration of netting by ectoplasm, which

TRUMPET MEDIUMS

passed through the veiling, and formed hands on the other side. (See his *Phenomena of Materialization*.) Nor can it be contended that red light introduced a necessary impediment, since many mediums sit in red lights: D. D. Home and Eusapia Palladino never sat in complete darkness. We can only conclude, therefore, that these particular tests were more than our medium could cope with.

Regarding red light, the following is of interest. We had planned to pass a beam of infra-red light in front of the medium, that is, between his body and the trumpets, which, if interfered with by the passage through it of a solid substance such as an arm, would indicate this on a registering apparatus. The light beam would thus act as a sort of astral thread, intangible yet real.

In order to try this, however, it was first of all necessary to ascertain whether or not the medium would see this light. One of the flashlight boxes was accordingly provided with an ordinary 60-watt bulb, instead of a flash bulb. The infra-red filter was in front of this, and shaded by a piece of cardboard, which permitted only a small square of light to escape through it. This box was placed on the far side of the room, behind the central table and the sitters' chairs, so as to be invisible to the medium. This light burned steadily throughout the sitting, but was neither seen nor commented upon by the medium! He was unaware of its existence, and hence did not object to it. It did not seem to interfere with the phenomena in any way.

At the next sitting, however, the box (arranged exactly as before) was placed so that he could see it. Cartheuser immediately objected, saying that the light would ruin the phenomena! After some slight controversy, the light was therefore extinguished and this test abandoned.

Before the first sitting, a number of faintly luminous

buttons had been attached to the walls and bookcases, the idea being that, if the medium passed in front of these buttons, they would be temporarily obscured by the passage of his body. Cartheuser immediately spotted these luminous points, however, and objected to them. They were accordingly removed and not used thereafter.

At the sitting when the net was employed, several quite revealing incidents occurred. Cartheuser was wearing, on that occasion, a large "turnip" watch, which was going. Mr. Silverberg, who was seated to the medium's right, heard the rustle of clothing, on several occasions, and was enabled to follow the movements of the medium through the ticking of his watch. He stated that the medium was constantly out of his chair, endeavoring in every way possible to pass between Silverberg and the netting cabinet, in order to gain access to its contents. Failing in this, he then endeavored to pass round *outside* the circle; that is, behind Mr. Silverberg. The latter moved his head back suddenly, and bumped into Cartheuser's stomach! He was immediately patted on the head by a hand, and the next instant the medium was back in his chair. He was convinced, however, that the medium was wandering about the room fairly constantly.

These observations of Silverberg's were confirmed by our own observations. It will be remembered that one of us (H. C.) was seated on the couch. From this position a tiny crack of light was visible under the front door, leading into the hall. Watching this streak of light carefully, one could see that it was partially or totally eclipsed on a number of occasions, by a solid body passing between it and the observer. In other words, these observations check with those of Silverberg, showing that the medium was constantly moving about the room on this occasion, evidently in his attempts to reach the interior of the netting cabinet.

Aside from the official sittings, a number of subsidiary tests were tried with Cartheuser on several afternoons. Experiments in telepathy were tried, using the regular Zener cards devised by Rhine. My wife and I alternated as agents, with Cartheuser as percipient. Both black and white and colored cards were tried. A number of runs failed to obtain anything beyond chance. Crystal gazing experiments yielded only negative results; the medium refused to try automatic writing.

Sealed boxes, containing unknown objects, were presented to him, to be held between his hands. We had hoped that he might gain some knowledge of their contents by means of clairvoyance. In this he failed completely.

Several tests were made to see whether the medium could discharge an electroscope without contact, by holding his fingers above it. No positive results were obtained— though this test had been successfully made with Palladino. (See my *Laboratory Investigations,* etc., p. 105.) Attempts to deflect the needle of a compass by means of the fingers were likewise negative, as were experiments with the sthenometer and other devices, intended to show radiations from the fingertips.

We had intended to try, in future sittings, galvanometer tests with this medium, to obtain his emotional reactions to certain leading questions, as we had previously tried with the medium Thomas Lacey in Toronto. We had also planned to obtain graphic tracings of the medium's pulse and respiration variations, during the sitting, on the kymograph; but these and other proposed tests were not tried, due to the somewhat abrupt termination of this series of séances. (Cartheuser left suddenly for Canada, and we never saw him again!)

It is most difficult to form a just estimate of the validity and significance of Cartheuser's phenomena, based on the limited number of sittings obtained by us (eight). This difficulty is enhanced by various contributory factors: the medium's innate timidity, his original fear of us (because of what had been said to him by mediums and spiritualists at Lily Dale and elsewhere), his aversion to tests (such as being tied or held), his aversion to light, and above all by the agreement we were forced to make with him (in order to induce him to sit for us at all)— that no tests would be made and no photographs taken without his prior consent and cooperation. It is of course absurd that a medium should be permitted to dictate the conditions prevailing at his sittings, since many mediums have willingly submitted to rigid tests from the start. However these were the conditions imposed by him, and we had to agree to them in order to induce him to sit at all. We feel that we adhered to our agreement throughout the series, and that the medium can have no possible cause for complaint on that score. He was treated kindly and sympathetically, and we even went out of our way to entertain and amuse him on many occasions. We cannot but feel that, if various tests had been carried out unknown to the medium, more conclusive results in various directions could have been obtained.

We feel that a high percentage of fraud enters into the production of Cartheuser's physical phenomena. Of that we have adequate evidence. He is alert and agile, capable of moving about with great rapidity, and with almost no noise. On a number of occasions he was undoubtedly out of his chair and moving about the room. Many of the trumpet phenomena might easily have been produced by him. The hands which produced the touches had every appearance of being his. We know that he

TRUMPET MEDIUMS

impressed the clay with a medal concealed in his pocket. When mechanical obstacles prevented him from reaching the trumpets and other objects placed in the netting cage, no voices and no phenomena of any kind took place.

Many of his phenomena might well have been produced fraudulently, though it must be admitted that we have no direct evidence that they *were* so produced. Among these may be included the small floating lights (perhaps a flashlight), the rapid circling of the metal microphone-stand by the trumpet or the luminous plate (which might have been accomplished by standing up and manipulating them from above), the simultaneous floating and tapping upon two trumpets at the same time, on opposite sides of the circle (which might have been produced by holding them in different hands and tapping upon them with a fingernail, both at the same time). We hesitate to assert that the phenomena in question *were* so produced in these various ways, during the séances in question, for we have no absolute proof that they were. But, in view of these possibilities, and his undoubtedly fraudulent actions on other occasions, and taking into account the axiom of science that the more parsimonious explanation is probably the true one, we should hesitate to conclude otherwise if pressed for an explanation of these particular phenomena.

While concluding, therefore, that the majority of his phenomena are explicable on the basis of fraud, there nevertheless remain certain instances which are most difficult to account for on this theory. Among these may be listed the touches at considerable distances (notably on Mr. Silverberg) when it seemed fairly certain that Cartheuser was in his chair; the occasion when the two voices spoke, seemingly simultaneously; other possible instances of a like character, and the ability of someone or something to see in the dark. These incidents remain extremely puzzling—quite aside from the mental phenomena, where supernormal information is seemingly obtained. We are quite convinced that a thorough and lengthy clinical, physical and psychological study of this medium would yield most interesting results, and it is regrettable that the limited number of our sittings, and the restricted conditions under which they were held, prevented this—which would require the active cooperation of several specialists in as many fields. It is our hope that some day this study may be undertaken.

We conclude, therefore, that Cartheuser presents an interesting case for study. His séances are often dramatic and entertaining, and contain items of genuine scientific interest. Many of his phenomena can be accounted for; but a small residuum remains which cannot readily be explained away, and this residuum presents a fascinating problem. This is especially true of his mental phenomena, in which information is sometimes given having every appearance of being definitely supernormal in character. Further experimentation is greatly to be desired here.

If it be felt that these tentative conclusions are disappointing and not sufficiently positive in character, it may be replied that eight sittings are not a large number upon which to form a just estimate of his case, and arrive at such positive decisions. The Psychological Institute of Paris sat with Eusapia Palladino for *four years* before bringing in their final verdict. The Committee comprised M. and Mme. Curie, M. d'Arsonval, M. Ballet, Prof. Charles Richet, M. Henri Bergson, Prof. Charpentier, M. Jules Courtier, and many others. They had at their disposal unlimited laboratory equipment, the cooperation of many scientific minds, and the services of the world's most powerful physical medium. If, under these circumstances, they nevertheless took four years in arriving at a final decision with regard to her phenomena, it must be admitted, we feel, that we cannot be criticized for arriving at only tentative conclusions in the present case. Moreover, we feel that certain conclusions *were* reached, and that much experience was gained, as the result of this series, which will prove useful in dealing with other mediums in the future. All in all, therefore, we conclude that our Cartheuser sittings proved valuable as well as interesting and provocative.

VII

THE INTRA-ATOMIC QUANTITY

IF IT COULD BE SHOWN, photographically and instrumentally, that something leaves the physical body at death, that would assuredly go a long way toward proving survival in some form—the persistence of some energy or entity, separate and apart from the functional activities of the body. Clairvoyants have said, on numerous occasions, that they have perceived some tenuous and subtle body leave at death; nurses and watchers at the bedsides of the dying have testified to like effect. Evidence of the survival of a mental principle has seemingly been obtained in messages of the communication type. And it has been contended that, theoretically, this mental principle must have an etheric vehicle of some sort through which to function. Nevertheless, biologists and physicists naturally desire some sort of laboratory proof of such an entity, and sporadic experiments which have been undertaken by them have led only to negative results. This, however, indicated little, as no systematic and serious experiments in this direction have ever been undertaken. Considering the theoretical importance of the problem, this in itself is astonishing.

Experiments undertaken from time to time by psychic students have likewise proved dubious and questionable, and subject to various interpretations. Many years ago Dr. Duncan MacDougall published some findings of his, in which small but appreciable losses of weight were noted at the moment of death, but others were unable to dupli-

THE INTRA-ATOMIC QUANTITY 95

cate his results and later experiments on animals proved negative. Dr. Baraduc, of Paris, published a strange book, *Mes Morts: Leurs Manifestations, Etc.,* in which he reproduced some photographs he had obtained while photographing his son's body every fifteen minutes for three hours after his death. These showed a misty ball of light which hovered over the body and finally disappeared. While no one has ever questioned Dr. Baraduc's sincerity, nevertheless his results seem never to have been taken very seriously, partly because they were never capable of being repeated by others, and partly because of the dubious character of the photographs themselves. With these exceptions, however, almost no attempts seem to have been made to obtain photographic or other evidence of the passage from the physical body of some entity at the moment of death—which again is somewhat surprising.

It was, therefore, with considerable interest that psychic students learned of the work which had been undertaken by the Director of the Dr. William Bernard Johnston Foundation for Biological Research, Dr. R. A. Watters, a physicist of standing. He succeeded, apparently, in photographing definite body-like (though cloudy and misty) forms over the bodies of animals which had just been killed in a specially constructed piece of apparatus known as a Wilson Chamber. In order that the reader may understand just what occurred, it will be necessary to go back to the beginning of this experimental work since it has a curious history.

The original suggestion upon which this series of experiments was based was embodied in a paper entitled *Physical and Psycho-Physiological Researches in Mediumship,* which I read before the First International Psychical Congress, Copenhagen, in 1921. I then said:

"Let us assume for the sake of argument that some such

entity as an 'astral body' exists, and that animals, as well as human beings, may possess such a vehicle. I shall further assume, merely for the sake of the experiment, that this astral body is driven out of the physical body by an anesthetic (which is of course the occult teaching). With these two tentative assumptions in mind, let us try the following experiment:

"Arrange a small box so as to imprison some animal— a dog, a cat or a small monkey. The box may be of aluminum, with a glass window, and must be hermetically sealed —except that an entrance pipe, provided with a stop-cock, must be fitted to admit air. This first box is suspended by means of four chains at its corners within a second box of glass, also hermetically sealed. The first box thus hangs suspended in the center of the second box. The pipe which is to admit air must of course pass to the outside of the larger box—the stop-cock being on the outside.

"The pipe which is to administer the anesthetic must also pass through the outer box into the inner one. An air-pump is also attached by means of a flexible pipe to the outer box, so that a stroke or two of the air-pump will reduce the air pressure within the outer box.

"Between these two boxes it is necessary to prepare an atmosphere of perfectly dust-free air or water vapor. Under these conditions we commence operations by admitting gas to the small box, so as to anesthetize the animal. At the same time, we gradually shut off the outer air supply. The anesthetic will, by hypothesis, displace the secondary or astral body of the imprisoned animal. This, in theory, must then occupy a position somewhere between the two boxes—that is, in the prepared atmosphere. But also, by hypothesis, it will generate rays of some description. These rays, of whatever nature they may ultimately prove to be, will cause ionization. Now, with a stroke or

THE INTRA-ATOMIC QUANTITY

two of the air-pump, we rapidly withdraw some of the air, causing the remaining air to expand suddenly. The temperature will immediately fall, and this will cause the water vapor to condense upon the ions. But the particles producing ionization have not a very extended range, at least some of them have not, and probably a variety of rays will be given off. Those particles of short range, then, will not produce ionization far from their source—that is, the astral body. Therefore, when condensation occurs, the resulting line will *outline the form of the astral body*. We shall have proved the existence of this body by thoroughly reliable, objective means. . . . Whatever one may think of this experiment, and whatever its outcome, I think that it is at least worth trying."

Such was the first, somewhat crude form in which this experiment was suggested. The apparatus actually employed in the tests, made years later, was of course far more complicated and delicate. Further, in these the specimens used were actually killed instead of being merely anesthetized—though smaller animals were utilized (mice, frogs and chicks). To these we shall come presently. First, however, a word regarding one or two of the terms employed, in order that lay-readers may follow the arguments and tests themselves.

Ionization: It is now generally known that an atom of matter consists essentially of a positive nucleus and a number of negative electrons which circle around it. In all neutral atoms these charges equal one another. If, however, an atom loses one of its electrons, then the positive charge on the nucleus overbalances the charge on the electrons and the atom becomes positive. If, on the other hand, an atom attaches to itself an electron, then the negative charge will overbalance the positive charge on the nucleus, and we have a negative atom. Such unbalanced atoms (electrically) are known as ions. The process is known as ionization.

It is possible to disrupt atoms experimentally by subjecting them to bombardment by particles moving at a terrific speed—such speed that they tear off one or more of the circling electrons. Radioactive compounds are the cannon generally used in such experiments, since they emit alpha, beta and gamma rays. The two former produce ionization in the atoms they hit.

Now, while no human eye can ever observe the swift flight of these alpha and beta particles, nevertheless their movements can be observed indirectly by means of a very ingenious apparatus known as a Wilson Chamber after its inventor, C. T. R. Wilson. This consists essentially of a hermetically sealed glass chamber filled with water vapor. In such a chamber the alpha and beta ray tracts can be seen (and photographed) because little droplets of water cling to the ions—just as, in a fog, a droplet of water will cling to a dust particle, thus creating the fog. The water droplets, in short, render temporarily visible the passage of the ionized particles, and hence the rays which produce such ionization. (The above is of course a very rough description of what occurs.)

Now, my idea when suggesting the original experiment was based upon such results: I postulated an astral body emitting some form of invisible rays, which rays might produce ionization in the water-vapor atmosphere into which (on theory) the astral body of the animal must pass at death (or perhaps under anesthetization). If such rays were close together, the water droplets would form about them as ionization occurred, and the result would somewhat resemble that noted on the outside of a glass of cold water on a very hot day. This misty cloud would take on the outline of the astral body of the

THE INTRA-ATOMIC QUANTITY 99

animal, and could be seen and photographed when it occurred. This summarizes very briefly the theory underlying the physics of the experiment.

Its biological aspect may be epitomized much more briefly. All psychic students are familiar with the general conception of the astral body, and the available evidence which has been adduced in its favor: certain types of apparitions and haunted houses, the experimental projection of such a body, and so on. Quite aside from the evidence afforded by psychic phenomena, however, certain biologists, as we know, have advanced a vitalistic theory of life, and one of them in particular, Mrs. Gaskell, in her book, *What Is Life?*, advanced the idea that there are, in the living body, two systems—which she termed the Y and Z systems respectively—one of which is purely material, while the other is immaterial, separating from the material system at death. This immaterial system normally dwells within the atoms of the material system; hence is intra-atomic. It is this intra-atomic quantity, she contends, which survives death.

Finally we come to the question of biological radiations. Much work has been done upon this, and it need only be said that while many biologists reject the evidence, there are also many who contend that the actuality of such radiations has been proved, pointing to the painstaking work of Gürwitsch, Otto Rahn, and many others in support of this. Many students of psychic phenomena have of course believed in the reality of such vital radiations largely because of certain supernormal physical phenomena which they have observed.

Piecing together now the above somewhat disjointed material, we have this: A Wilson Cloud Chamber is a device for showing ionization and rendering the process photographable. If some entity or quantity leaves the physical body at death, itself emitting rays, this entity should on theory produce ionization in its immediate vicinity; and if this occurred, then the entity might perhaps be caught and photographed at the moment of its passage. This was the basic idea underlying my original suggestion in 1921 to the First International Psychic Congress.

Some ten years elapsed before it was put to actual test. I myself did not possess the necessary equipment, which is enormously complicated and expensive, nor did I feel that I possessed the highly technical knowledge necessary to undertake this work. It was at this precise juncture that Dr. R. A. Watters and I began our correspondence, which continued for many years. I saw in him a man eminently suited to undertake the task, a trained physicist, an X-ray specialist, an expert photographer, a scientist interested in psychic phenomena, and also possessed of an open mind and a quantity of beautiful apparatus suitable for the investigation in view. He undertook the work with energy and enthusiasm.

Utilizing a specially constructed Wilson Chamber, he experimented upon frogs, grasshoppers, mice and chicks. At first he employed ether and electricity as lethal agents, but found both of these unsatisfactory for the reason that it was impossible to tell the exact moment of death of the specimen—a very important item. He later constructed within the chamber a miniature guillotine, capable of decapitating the animal instantaneously (after being anesthetized). This enabled the exact moment of death to be determined.

Photographs taken of the interior of the chamber produced some very interesting and curious results. The body of the dead animal was shown in its mist-filled interior; but in that mist, separate and apart from the physical body, a cloud-like form was also revealed, hover-

THE INTRA-ATOMIC QUANTITY 101

ing in space. This seemed to conform in general outline to the specimen's body. Certainly this outline was very tenuous and uncertain; it seemed to be a fog within a fog. Nevertheless, *something* was present. Of the initial fifty photographs taken, fourteen were positive, in that they showed some cloud-like mass in the fog. In the remaining thirty-six (when no shadows were seen) the animal failed to recover in ten instances, and did recover in twenty-six. In the early experiments before the guillotine had been installed, Dr. Watters considered it highly significant that the cloud-like mass was only detected when the specimen was actually dead, and was never photographed when the specimen recovered. This seemed to show that death was a necessary factor.

The upshot of this preliminary investigation was to convince Dr. Watters that something very significant had been detected, and that there was at least a *prima facie* case for the existence of some intra-atomic quantity, or something very analogous to it. He published these preliminary findings in his pamphlet, *The Intra-atomic Quantity*.

A year or two later a series of analogous experiments was undertaken under the auspices of Dr. Nandor Fodor's International Institute for Psychical Research in London by Mr. B. J. Hopper, the results being published in a pamphlet entitled, *Enquiry into the Cloud Chamber Method of Studying the Intra-atomic Quantity*. His findings were entirely negative, in that he failed to obtain the cloud-like forms which Dr. Watters had observed; he also criticized the technique employed in the original experiments. In a printed reply to this, Dr. Watters pointed out that identical methods had not in fact been employed on both occasions, and insisted that it was unfair to compare negative with positive results while such differences existed. Further correspondence ensued of a highly technical character, into which it is unnecessary to enter now. The net result was to leave the question unsettled, with the controversialists divided into two hostile camps.

Dr. Watters continued his investigations, however, utilizing more and more refined and highly complicated apparatus. These results were later published in a booklet entitled *Cloud Chamber Investigations Into Post-Mortem Ions.* (This was written jointly with Dr. William Bernard Johnston, and issued as Bulletin III of their Foundation.)

Several different cloud chambers were employed among which were the original machine, now entitled the Jenkins-Wilson chamber, and the Carrington-Wilson chamber, so named because it conformed most closely to the device originally suggested by me in my Congress paper. As ultimately developed by Dr. Watters, however, this was an enormously complicated and elaborate machine, differing from the original infant about as widely as a modern printing press differs from a page of hand-set type! Much of this bulletin is devoted to a detailed description of these various pieces of apparatus, and would doubtless prove boring and unintelligible to the lay-reader. The question is: What was the upshot of these newer investigations?

Very briefly, the results may perhaps be stated as follows: Clouds and cloud-like masses were indeed noted on various occasions, and observed or photographed, but these seemed to be due to causes other than the intra-atomic quantity originally supposed. It was found that gaseous ions were liberated from organisms during post-mortem chemical changes, due to glycolysis, fermentation, and so forth. Also that cloud-forms resulted from the accumulation of gases in the specimen chamber, behind

THE INTRA-ATOMIC QUANTITY 103

the cellophane window, which gases during expansion were transmitted by the cellophane into eddy-currents, jets of gas, and a cloud atmosphere of uneven temperature. Such eddy-currents were also found to exist in the case of the Locher apparatus.

When, however, the most refined and perfected apparatus was employed, and such sources of possible error eliminated, no cloud-effects were observed resembling in contour the specimens killed—as had been observed in the earlier experiments. In short, the striking results formerly noted were shown to have been due to technical faults in the apparatus, plus certain highly complicated post-mortem chemical changes, especially gases, which served as the bases for cloud nuclei. Dr. Watters thus succeeded in identifying the nature of the death-cloud, as well as its origin and characteristics, and from the point of view of the study of certain phenomena associated with the deaths of lower animals, this is an exceedingly valuable and interesting contribution. On the other hand, he has apparently shown that the more striking and dramatic characteristics did not in fact exist—or rather that those which had been noted were due to faulty technique, and did not actually represent any intra-atomic quantity in the sense they were originally supposed to. In brief, these results were negative insofar as they showed the normal physico-chemical causation of the death-clouds formerly observed, proving that they were not due to the passage of any intra-atomic quantity at the moment of death, in the sense that this represented anything superphysical or psychic.

In one sense of course this is a disappointing result to those who hoped that something more positive had been obtained—a series of experiments which had at last definitely proved the emergence from the body of some subtle principle or vehicle at death. However, quite aside from the intrinsic value of these experiments in throwing light upon the nature of death, as they do, there still remain, it seems to me, some interesting and not altogether explained results. Among these are the striking resemblances which undoubtedly exist between the death-cloud and the body of the specimen in the original experiments, and the fact that such clouds were only observed when the animal had actually died, and never when the animal was capable of resuscitation (stressed by Dr. Watters in his first report). It is now contended that such resemblances were purely coincidental, but one cannot help wondering why the death-cloud of a mouse, for example, never resembled that of a frog or a grasshopper, and vice versa. May there not still be some X, some unexplained residuum present in these experiments, which might be shown to exist when photographing the results in infra-red or ultra-violet light, employing quartz lenses, perhaps? Such experiments have, as we know, yielded some striking results in other cases; might it not be possible that they would in these instances also? At least it would seem that such experiments should be tried, for the results on any theory would prove both valuable and interesting.

More than twenty years have elapsed since such experiments were first suggested, and more than eight years of intensive work have been devoted to them in the modern laboratory. If all this has proved nothing else, it has at least proved the vast amount of painstaking investigation necessary in order to settle a problem in psychical research, and the utter futility of trying to settle such problems in the absence of proper laboratory equipment. No mere amateur dabbling in this subject can hope to throw light upon its ultimate problems. Adequately endowed and equipped psychic laboratories are absolutely necessary, if we are ever to hope to place psychical research upon the **same level of respectability as the other official sciences.**

VIII

EXPERIMENTS I SHOULD LIKE TRIED AT MY OWN DEATH

AFTER ALL, there is no reason why we should not regard death as a perfectly natural process, just as we regard birth. It is a most interesting and significant process too. At birth we are ushered into a new world—a world of living physical organisms. There are many who feel that our final passing is but another birth, this time into a *mental* world, just as real and vital as this one.

Does such a mental realm seem incredible to you? We enter one every night in our dreams, when we meet and converse with people, and when we perceive houses, tables, chairs, rivers, valleys, which appear just as real to us as those we encounter in waking life, and which no possible test we can devise will prove otherwise. Rap on a dream-table and it is hard; throw a stone through a dream-window and it will be broken!

There *is* a psychic world, therefore, which may seem just as real to its inhabitants as does this physical world to us; and this potential sphere has been characterized by some delvers into the occult as a rationalized dream world.

It is this mental world which we are thought to enter at death. Certainly our physical bodies do not accompany us; they remain here, and if they are not properly tended soon disintegrate. They are mere shells which we have cast aside, like a suit of clothing. They are not the persons we knew and loved. You *are* not your body; you *inhabit* your body. In passing, it is left behind.

Hundreds of unemotional and scientifically-minded persons have left their bodies to medical schools, for the benefit of the research studies of young doctors. This is a fine, unselfish gesture, but it is not new; it has been done times without number. Personally, being a psychical researcher, I should like to try some novel tests—tests which might perhaps throw light upon the nature of life, as well as death; tests which would include not alone the physical structure of man but also his mind and consciousness.

All psychic students have been impressed by the curious way in which supernormal phenomena cluster around the moment of death. Visions at the time are by no means uncommon. Often these visions accurately depict events which may actually be transpiring at the time. Flashes of extraordinary memory have frequently been noted. Apparitions of the dying person have been seen by others (many hundreds of miles distant) who were totally unaware of the fatal illness or accident. Strange occurrences of all kinds have been experienced and recorded.

If death represents the extinction of consciousness, it is difficult for us to understand why these phenomena should occur. But if our transition represents merely the *withdrawal* of consciousness, then such extended powers become at least intelligible. As Dr. Alexis Carrel remarked, "Man overflows and is greater than the organism which he inhabits."

But this surviving mind of ours, granting its persistence, must surely inhabit a body of some sort. It can be no mere Euclidian point-in-space. It is said to inhabit some sort of etheric body, which acts as the mind's vehicle upon the mental plane—just as our physical body acts as its vehicle upon the physical plane. This body is not the soul, but merely the vehicle for its expression.

We psychic students have accumulated a mass of striking evidence tending to prove the reality of such a subtle body—the spiritual body of St. Paul. We have also collected much evidence tending to show the persistence of individual human consciousness. But much *more* evidence is desirable—to be tested and checked, whenever possible, by modern instruments of precision, such as those employed in the modern laboratory. Such are the tests *I* should like to have made at the time of my *own* passing.

What sort of experiments could be made at such a time? Those gifted with psychic sight (clairvoyants) have, it is true, described the process in detail; but we want more objective evidence than this. We should like, if possible, instrumental proofs that *something* leaves the body at the moment of death; and, if that could be proved, we should have not only a stumbling block for materialistic physiology, but also a strong presumption that some mental entity used or inhabited this etheric body—thus constituting proof of human survival.

Students of the occult have for long contended that there is an atmosphere or aura surrounding the human body, and chemical screens have been devised in order to render it visible to the human eye. Dr. Walter J. Kilner, of St. Thomas' Hospital, London—who wrote a book upon the subject—employed dicyanin, a coal-tar product, which seemingly rendered the human eye sensitive to vibrations beyond the visible spectrum—probably in the ultra-violet. At all events, by the aid of these screens, many persons were enabled to perceive what they described as the aura, and a considerable number of physicians utilized this method for diagnosis. Kilner asserted that the aura, clearly perceptible in life, rapidly faded at death, so that the inanimate body possessed *no* aura. If verified, this would represent an interesting physiological phenomenon, though it would of course not bear directly on the problem of survival.

Closely allied to these are certain experiments made by Dr. Elmer Gates, in which he passed electric waves of certain intensities and frequencies through the bodies of animals. He found that, while the living tissues permitted the passage of the rays, those of the dead animal blocked their transmission. This he considered an excellent test of death, but it is not of course a proof of anything psychic in man.

It is possible, however, that a body placed in a powerful electric field might show interesting results, perhaps supplying "carrier waves" for other energies. Some psychic students have experimented with a device known as a lastrometer, which is intended to show the accumulation of energy during a séance. It is possible that this instrument might show some energy liberated by the body at the moment of death, and should certainly be tried.

French researchers have claimed that calcium sulphide screens will glow with added brilliance when an etheric or astral body approaches them. This added brilliance (and that of the plate in the lastrometer above mentioned) might be detected by means of sensitive photo-electric cells. I for one should like this experiment undertaken.

Then there is an instrument which I devised many years ago, called the howler, because it emits a howling sound when any body (physical body) approaches it. It was primarily built for use in séances, the idea being that if the medium is known to be in his chair (held there) and the howler nevertheless emits characteristic sounds, it would be proof that some invisible energy or entity was in the immediate environment of the coil, influencing the electric current circulating through it. Some invisible

EXPERIMENTS I SHOULD LIKE TRIED

energy or entity, projected from the body at death, might perhaps affect the coil in a similar manner. It would at least be worth trying.

Infra-red and ultra-violet light might be impinged upon the body at the time. I am strongly of the belief that interesting and unknown changes take place in the immediate vicinity of the subject's body during death, and these should certainly be studied, as throwing light upon the process, if only from the physiological point of view.

If the experiments with the Wilson Cloud Chamber had proved more conclusive, these would be most interesting to try—using a specially built, large chamber for the purpose. Perhaps some similar device may be invented, yielding more positive results; and, if this were the case, I should certainly like to try some such experiment, when the time arrived for it to be tried!

I should therefore like to offer myself as a sort of psychic guinea pig, and I feel assured that such tests would prove most fascinating. Were sufficient money and interest forthcoming, such researches could readily be made—not in one single case, but in hundreds and thousands of cases. Many striking and suggestive facts might well result in consequence. Should not our motto be—like that of the old Roman gladiators—"We who are about to die, salute you!"

IX

POLTERGEIST PHENOMENA

ALL PSYCHIC STUDENTS are familiar with so-called poltergeist cases, concerning which much has been written. They represent cases of bizarre, spontaneous physical phenomena, in which bells are rung, crockery broken, objects thrown about, and so on, for no assignable cause. Frequently they occur in the presence of children, and, in some cases as we know, these children have been caught throwing the objects and producing fraudulent phenomena, so that, in the opinion of many students of our subject, it would seem probable that *all* such cases are to be accounted for by these simple means. This, it will be remembered, was the opinion of Mr. Frank Podmore, who contributed an article upon the subject to the *Proceedings* S.P.R., Volume XII.

Recently, however, I have had occasion to collect and analyze a large number of such cases, and I have been surprised to find the relatively small proportion of them in which trickery was actually detected. In a bulletin, I summarized some 318 historic poltergeist cases, running back to the year 530 A.D. and continuing in an almost unbroken stream until the year 1935.* They have been reported from every part of the civilized and uncivilized world, from every country and clime, and the general characteristics of the phenomena were found to be remarkably similar and uniform.

---

*Several interesting cases have been reported since, but are not included in the above summary.

POLTERGEIST PHENOMENA

Analyzing the reports thus rendered—some poorly observed, others well evidenced—I have found that twenty-two of them were undoubtedly fraudulent, in that trickery was actually detected. Eighteen of them were doubtful cases, in that they were inconclusive, or trickery might possibly have been operative. Assuming that *all* these doubtful cases were fraudulent, and adding this number to the proved cases, we nevertheless find that this represents a total of forty in all, while the number of unexplained cases equals 278.

Thus, we find that only about one-eighth of all the reported instances have ever been adequately explained, while seven-eighths of them have remained unexplained to the present day. This is assuredly very different from the seemingly prevailing conception that practically *all* such cases have been proved to be fraudulent!

Were poltergeists merely due to trickery, on the one hand, and credulity and superstition, on the other, we should assuredly expect to find them in greater numbers in relatively uncivilized countries, or at least in those in which the level of culture is not high.

But an examination of the material shows that precisely the reverse of this is in fact the case—England, France, Italy, Germany and the United States having the greatest number, while countries such as Haiti, China, Barbados and Transylvania have the least. This is certainly surprising. The actual figures, based on the 318 cases collected and published, are as follows:

	Number of Cases
Great Britain	101
France	57
United States	54
Germany	27

	Number of Cases
Italy	14
India	7
Norway and Sweden, Hungary, Russia	6
Iceland, Austria, South Africa	4
Spain, Jamaica	3
Java, China, Sumatra	2
Barbados, Martinique, Switzerland, Haiti, Argentina, Chile, Portugal, Bolivia, Belgium, Madagascar, Czechoslovakia, Ceylon, Brazil, Greece, Transylvania (each)	1

How are these results to be explained?

Certainly, they may be explained in part by assuming that—in England, for example—the press is highly efficient and well organized, and that anything unusual is likely to be reported in the newspapers immediately, while in countries lacking these facilities similar cases are likely to go unrecorded and unreported.

But this would only bear out my contention that the number of such cases, if known, would be exceedingly large, and would probably run into the thousands instead of the hundreds. How account for these thousands of cases? And is it probable that, in all ages of the world and in every country, thousands of spurious phenomena should occur precisely similar in character? That, for example, in Iceland they should be the same as in Sumatra, and a thousand years ago the same as today?

It may be contended, of course, that imitation plays a part here, and that if one case is reported in the papers, it might act as an incentive to other naughty little girls and boys to do likewise: hence the greater number of cases in those countries having an efficient press.

But an examination of the material does not seem to bear out this theory. Very rarely are similar disturbances

POLTERGEIST PHENOMENA 113

noted in the same locality or in the same period; they are usually fairly widely separated and many years apart. Even should such reports find their way into the newspapers, one can hardly believe that an account of a poltergeist noted in South Wales in 1877 could have influenced a child to imitate it in Plymouth in 1913. I think we may safely leave this factor out of account, save perhaps in very few instances.

The greater number of cases would thus seem to indicate that more of them have found their way into the press, and not that more of them have occurred. It seems to me highly probable that numbers of them have occurred all over the world, but that they have never been reported. Is it not remarkable that such manifestations should have occurred in every civilized and uncivilized country, in all ages, and that they should bear this striking similarity?

My own opinion is that the last word has by no means been said concerning poltergeists, and that an impartial survey of the historic evidence furnishes us with a good *prima facie* case for the existence of such phenomena, which would thus represent instances of genuine supernormal physical manifestations of a spontaneous character.

Once this be granted, we can turn our attention to a study of their nature and the casual factors involved. This study should, I believe, occupy the attention of psychic students in the future.

While the above is I believe true, it is of course also true that some of these curious cases are due to trickery and fraud, either conscious or unconscious. There is some evidence that spurious phenomena have sometimes been produced by normally honest individuals in a state of semi-dissociation, in which state they were partially or wholly unconscious of the actions they were performing. In other cases there seems to have been a compulsion to commit fraud; and the psychological aspects of these cases are very interesting. It is to be hoped that a detailed study of some of them may be undertaken one day in the future.

The following case is perhaps illustrative of what I have just said, while it presents the interesting feature of having been cured by means of suggestion. It occurred some thirty years ago, and I wrote a report on it at the time. This report I now quote, since it gives the details of the case. It runs as follows:

On September 27th, 1917, I received a telephone call from Mrs. P., frantically asking me to visit her as soon as possible, to observe a number of striking phenomena which, she said, were then actively manifesting. I called about three hours later in the early evening and found that manifestations were still in progress. Mrs. P. received me cordially, and I found that she, her nurse, and three small children were temporarily living in a furnished apartment in New York, which they had taken to escape the activities of the poltergeist, which had made their lives unbearable in their country home.

The three children were: Jewell, aged ten; Edith, aged six; and Barbara, aged three. Mrs. P. herself was in a highly excited state of mind, as was also her nurse and companion, Miss G.—a sensible, gray-haired lady of perhaps fifty, who had been the constant companion of Mrs. P. for seven or eight years, and in whom she had implicit confidence.

Both Mrs. P. and Miss G. were evidently greatly agitated over the state of affairs; so much so, indeed, that neither of them had obtained a good night's sleep for several weeks. It was obvious from the first that if any normal explanation were to be found or any trickery discovered, Mrs. P. and Miss G., and the two younger children, might safely be left out of consideration—the latter because of their youth and implicit belief in the phenomena; the former because of their shattered nerves and evident excitement and sincerity.

Little Jewell was, however, a questionable factor. She appeared to me to be a highly sensitive, alert, precocious child for her age, full of mischief, and certainly capable of producing a great variety of tricks, should the temptation to do so present itself. Mrs. P. assured me, however, that a number of phenomena had taken place in Jewell's absence—which obviously complicated matters. At the time I arrived the children were being put to bed by Miss G., the nurse, and phenomena in the rooms occupied by us had ceased. Mrs. P. told me that they seemed to center about the children, and largely about Jewell.

The door of the bedroom had been left slightly ajar, and once or twice we heard thumps and bumps issuing from the room—as though small objects were being thrown about. Suddenly, through the crack left by the door being slightly ajar, I perceived a blanket, which had been placed over the head of the bed, suddenly snatched away as though by an invisible hand. It sailed through the air and landed on the floor of the bedroom— and, so far as I could see at the time, neither Miss G. nor any of the children had had an opportunity to touch it.

More noise issuing from the room. Mrs. P. and I then stood in the doorway, pushing it open so that we could have a full view of the room and its occupants. Prior to this, several small objects, such as a toy horse and a doll, had fallen to the floor; but all manifestations ceased promptly the moment we stood in the doorway, and did not begin again that evening.

I remained chatting with Mrs. P. for some considerable

time after this, hoping that phenomena of some sort would take place. They failed, however, to put in an appearance. Mrs. P. told me that they had been unable to keep anything in place in the house. Objects were thrown off the table, fruit thrown about the room, and several oranges and pears, which had been on the sideboard, had completely disappeared; towels were thrown in the bath; the clay in which the children had been working was thrown about the room, and other manifestations of a similar character had frequently been seen.

The following day I called on Mrs. P. and she told me that the phenomena had continued more or less as before —only more limited in their activity—and she then begged me to go down with them to their country home and spend the night and endeavor to discover, if possible, the cause of the manifestations. Mrs. P. told me that she had constantly felt a presence about the house; that poltergeist phenomena of a typical character had constantly annoyed them for several weeks past, and that she wished a stop put to the manifestations if possible. I suggested that a clairvoyant should accompany me, so that we could discover—possibly by psychic means if not by physical—the cause of these phenomena. To this Mrs. P. readily agreed, and accordingly, on the evening of September the 29th, Mr. X. and myself went to Mount Vernon and remained there overnight, returning the following afternoon.

One particular room in the P. house was said to be more especially haunted than the others. This was a small, empty room at the back of the house, devoid of furniture, and rather thickly laden with dust—having been quite unused for a number of months past. When Mr. X. and myself arrived, the children had gone to bed and were sound asleep; we did not see anything of them until the following morning. At 2.00 a.m., phenomena of any sort having failed to put in an appearance, Mrs. P., Mr. X. and myself held an impromptu séance in the haunted room. We sat around a small table, which had been brought in for the purpose, completely darkened the room, and remained there until long past three, in an attempt to obtain phenomena of some sort, or some inkling as to their nature. No manifestations of any kind were observed, however, and toward four o'clock we went to bed—disappointed in our investigation.

The next day a few odd phenomena took place, but they were always under such conditions that they might possibly have been produced fraudulently by the oldest girl, who was a typical "poltergeist child," and nothing conclusive one way or the other could be obtained.

A day or two later, Mrs. P. again came to town, having once more been driven from her home, she asserted, by the activity of the ghost. Mrs. P. telephoned us, and Mr. X. and myself went down to the house; but no phenomena occurred during our visit. After about an hour I had to leave to attend to other matters, but Mr. X. remained to see if anything further could be discovered. After a further wait, during which no phenomena occurred, Mr. X. went to the telephone and pretended to call a number. The telephone was so situated that it was just beyond visual reach from the room occupied by the children, but, by leaning well back in the hallway, a slight glimpse of this room could be obtained.

After calling the number, Mr. X. placed his head in such a position that a slanting view of a portion of the room could be obtained, and, during the few seconds that he obtained this view, he saw little Jewell seize an orange from the sideboard, fling it across the room, and quickly fold her hands again in her lap. This was when the attention of the others was distracted, and she had two or three seconds of absolute freedom. The net result was that her hands were folded in her lap, and she wore an aspect of complete innocence by the time the orange fell to the floor; and this "phenomenon" brought forth the usual cries of surprise from Mrs. P., the nurse, and the other children.

Mr. X. called Mrs. P. into an adjoining room and told her that he was convinced that the majority of the phenomena, if not all of them, had been produced normally by the little girl, Jewell, and that she alone was the cause of the phenomena. He stated that it might be possible that she had been impressed to do all this by other intelligences than her own, but that the actual phenomena themselves were produced by her muscles and hands in an ordinary manner. Mrs. P. refused to believe this—stating that many manifestations had occurred which Jewell could not have produced; and the result of a rather sharp interview was that Mr. X. left, having failed to convince Mrs. P. that the manifestations were produced normally.

The following day, and the day after, I again visited Mrs. P., and on several occasions I also caught little Jewell throwing objects about, and producing ghostly phenomena in a way which left no doubt of the fact that she herself was the sole source of the manifestations; and, judging by the dexterity with which she performed the actions, it was very evident that she had long practiced them, and that, doubtless, she alone was the cause of all the phenomena which had occurred.

Feeling that an abrupt statement to this effect would leave Mrs. P. as unconvinced as before, judging by Mr. X.'s experience, I refrained from saying anything at the time; and, in order to convince myself more thoroughly, and establish the case more clearly in my own mind, I paid

POLTERGEIST PHENOMENA 119

two or three more visits to the apartment, and also again visited their country home, spending a day and another night there to insure the accuracy of my own observations.

The result of all this was to convince myself more fully than ever that the little girl Jewell was in fact the sole cause of all the phenomena so far witnessed; and that those phenomena which had been asserted to occur in her absence were due to the fact that objects had been thrown through the open door into another room, by her, and their production in an empty room thus fully explained.

I then told Mrs. P. the conclusions to which I had been driven, and she was forced to accept the evidence as more or less conclusive. She was loath to believe, however, that the little girl had consistently tricked her in this manner; whereupon I suggested that it might be interesting to try and "cure" the case by a somewhat novel method. Merely confronting the child with the evidence would probably have brought forth a denial, and the "phenomena" would have continued, after a brief intermission.

The most interesting part of the case now follows. On the evening of October the second, I called upon Mrs. P. after the children had been put to bed and were all sound asleep. Sitting by the bedside of little Jewell, I made a number of passes over her forehead, without contact, *willing* that she should fall into a deep sleep in which she would be susceptible to suggestion.

After two or three minutes she seemed partially to awaken. An active opposition had doubtless been set up to these suggestions in her dream-consciousness, and this was so manifest that one hand was stretched out as though she were warding off some influence she did not like. I thereupon waited for two or three minutes, until she once again sank into a sound sleep, when I resumed the passes and suggestions.

This time she seemed to fall into a heavier sleep, and I continued the suggestions for about ten minutes before administering any therapeutic suggestions, as one might call them in this case. After I was fully assured that the child was in a receptive mood, I suggested to her that she would have no more desire to perform tricks; that she no longer wished to mystify her mother and nurse; that every time she picked up an article, with the object of throwing it, she would feel an influence restraining her from doing so. I kept up these suggestions for a good twenty minutes, hammering them into the subconscious, and ended by the usual suggestion that she should awaken without any memory of what had occurred.

This was on Tuesday. On Friday evening, Mrs. P. telephoned me, saying that since the treatment no phenomena of any character had developed; and that they seemed to have stopped entirely. The child seemed to have quieted down, and was in better health and spirits than before. Things went along like this for about a week, when minor manifestations again developed. A second treatment of the above character had the effect of completely curing the girl. Thereafter no further manifestations of any character were observed.

This case is interesting, I think, in that it offers us a suggestion as to a possible basis for the treatment and cure of cases of this character, when caught "red-handed," and the subject is susceptible to suitable suggestion.*

* Since the above was written, two valuable contributions have been made to the literature of Poltergeist cases. The first is Dr. Nandor Fodor's psychoanalysis of a poltergeist girl (or rather woman), which throws great light upon the psychological (unconscious) factors involved. The second is Mr. Harry Price's book *Poltergeist Over England,* which summarizes some 500 cases, concluding that the majority of them are undoubtedly genuine and supernormal. This agrees entirely with my own conclusion—despite negative cases such as the above—that genuine Poltergeist cases undoubtedly exist, though their explanation is yet to be found.

X

HOW SPIRIT PICTURES ARE FAKED

From a normal photographic point of view, almost any type of accident which ruins a negative has been attributed to the mysterious activities of the spirit world. Flare, reticulation, inconsistent chemical action of developers, light streaks—all these unpleasant little things, and many more, have been seized upon by unscrupulous mediums as evidence that images of unearthly presences have registered upon the emulsion.

To this list of errors have been added all the wily and diabolical photographic tricks known, in order to produce spirit pictures. Armed with the common photographic fallacy that the camera doesn't lie, frauds set about duping gullible persons who are grieving for deceased loved ones.

Spirit photography, so-called, has a long and an interesting history. It goes back eighty years, to William H. Mumler, of Boston, who was prosecuted for fraud in 1868. He was followed by Edouard Buguet, in France, and (in England) by David Duguid, William Hope, Mrs. Ada E. Deane, the Falconer brothers, John Myers, and (in the U.S.A.) by William M. Keeler, and many others. All these mediums were caught at one time or another, in their varied careers, in deliberate fraud. Several of them were prosecuted.

In the present chapter I cannot enter into controversial matters, nor into the history of the subject, interesting as this would be. I propose instead to detail some of the ingenious trick photographic methods which have been employed by fraudulent mediums in the past. By these methods they obtained spirit faces (or extras, as they call them) on the negative in addition to the image of the person who sat for his picture.

Two of the simplest and most obvious methods are double exposure and double printing. It will hardly be necessary for me to take time on these. Every amateur photographer is familiar with the results so obtained. In fact, he undoubtedly uses these methods in making montages or in getting special effects. The spirit pictures thus produced are legion.

Another ingenious method of obtaining spirit faces is by means of a device referred to as a ghost stamp. It has the advantage of being workable even under the eyes of a skeptical committee. A small, flat box, capable of being palmed in the hand, is employed. The upper part contains a miniature battery and an electric pea-lamp. Over a small opening in the bottom of the box is glued a tiny positive transparency. The circuit is closed by pressing upon a spring. Pressed against the sensitized surface of a plate in the darkroom, it will print a perfect vignetted extra on the emulsion. It takes but a second to operate, and the box can be concealed again instantly, allowing the hands to be shown empty.

Peculiar markings and cloud-like forms are readily put on plates by using an unevenly mixed developer. A heavy, concentrated, one-solution developer is generally used. About one-quarter ounce of the developer is poured into a graduated measure, and four ounces of water are added slowly by letting it gently trickle down the inside of the glass. The two liquids—owing to the difference in specific gravity—do not mix, the concentrate remaining at the bottom of the vessel. The unmixed solution is then poured

HOW SPIRIT PICTURES ARE FAKED

slowly over the exposed sensitized plate. The image slowly develops, and, in addition, cloud-like markings of great density make their appearance upon the plate. These markings often assume very curious forms and can, with a little imagination, be seen as heads and so forth.

Another and still better method often used is to drop a small crystal (not much larger than a pin's head) of sodium thiosulfate upon a plate during the process of development. The crystal slowly dissolves, producing weird markings. Many other chemicals will produce the same results.

It is also possible to obtain a recognizable face, using the sitter's own camera, marked plates, and other devices, and while the latter stands over the photographer-medium in the darkroom. A backed plate is used, "in order to cut out halation." After the plate has been in the developer for a short time, it is taken out and examined, "to see if anything has yet developed." This is a natural procedure and arouses no suspicion. In the act of doing so, however, the medium carefully rubs away with his finger a portion of the backing at the spot where he wants the head to appear. He then returns the plate to the tray for another brief period of development. During this time, however, the medium has secured and now holds between his fingers a small film positive. He again takes out the plate and holds it up once more, "to see how things are progressing." This time he slips the film behind the plate, so that it covers the spot previously rubbed away. It is held up to the safety lamp for inspection.

Enough time is allowed to print the face, which will come out quite clearly. The backing prevents the rest of the plate from becoming fogged, and the result is a fine extra obtained under real "test conditions"!

Another method, said to have been used by Keeler,

was to produce extras upon the sensitized plate by means of a bright image reflected through his studio window into the lens of his camera. Heads were cut out of bright tinfoil and pasted on boards covered with dead-black paper. These were hung at suitable angles outside the studio window, so as to be reflected into the lens. The result was flare spots on the negative. Mr. Harry Price of London and others have experimented with this method and have reported very striking results.

There are of course innumerable methods by which one film or plate can be *substituted* for another during the sitting. The plate itself may be switched, or the plate-holder and all. Obvious markings for purposes of identification can be imitated.

Perhaps the best way to mark a photographic plate secretly is by means of x-rays. A pattern or image can be recorded on the emulsion without even opening the film package. If the plate has been substituted, this will certainly disclose the fact. There will be no x-ray markings on the plate you ultimately receive from the medium. A stencil should be used allowing the x-rays to imprint a definite pattern on the plate. This method was used some years ago in England, and one of the best-known spirit photographers in the world was exposed in consequence.

But x-rays, infra-red rays, ultra-violet light, and radio-active salts of various kinds may be employed by the fraudulent spirit photographers, too, in order to produce striking effects upon the films or plates. For example, radioactive sulfide of zinc may be used in a variety of ways. Images may be painted on the plate wrapper, using this preparation, and these will be clearly impressed upon the plate if they are allowed to remain in contact for some little time. A face painted on the inside of the plate-holder will reproduce itself upon the plate.

HOW SPIRIT PICTURES ARE FAKED

Some years ago a spirit photographer employed a method very similar to the above, which eluded detection for some time. He used the sitter's own plates, and every step in the development was carried out by the investigator himself. Nevertheless a beautiful extra appeared upon the examined and marked plate!

He asked the sitter, first of all, to write his name upon the plate, so as to identify it. While the sitter was doing this, the medium extracted from his pocket a small newspaper cut, which he had painted over with radio-active paint. This he held in his left hand. He then asked to be allowed to sign the plate also. While doing so, he held his cupped left hand (containing the newspaper cut) over the plate, and by the time he had finished writing his name the radioactive paint had made an impression on the emulsion. The sitter could then take complete charge of the plate, but the trick was already done; the extra already upon the plate. This method was quite ingenious, but was ultimately detected.

Sketches, old photographs and illustrations, may of course be copied and used in double exposure or double printing. They are first of all cut from the paper and placed upon a dead-black background. They are then photographed in the ordinary way—underexposed a little and a fuzz of cotton placed round them to soften the edges and supply the necessary ectoplasm. The prepared plate must then be substituted for the sitter's own plate at some appropriate time, and *this* plate then marked for identification. The extra then appears upon the plate which the sitter has just examined and initialed, or otherwise marked.

One great drawback to this method, however, is that when an illustration is copied, the incriminating dot-formation of the half-tone screen also appears on the photograph. If this be examined microscopically the fraud is revealed, thus giving away its earthly origin. In order to eliminate this, mediums have rubbed the original halftone with a stick of soft wax. This combines with the printing ink, smudges the picture slightly, and does away with the tell-tale dots.

Another clever trick, sometimes employed, is to paint or draw an extra upon the emulsion of the plate (before exposure), using for this purpose a pigment composed of a mixture of glycerin, gum arabic, sugar, water, and a yellow dye. This is quite invisible when the plate is examined in the red light of the darkroom. When the sitter's portrait is taken, this also appears in the finished product, and represents the usual spirit face peering over the sitter's shoulder.

But the tricks of the fraudulent medium are many, and it would require a book, rather than a brief summary, to expose all of them. The expert trickster is usually just one step ahead of any but the most skilled and cautious investigator. One may supply his own camera, his own marked films or plates, take the pictures himself, develop them himself, and yet be swindled! Only a thorough knowledge of photography, magic, trickery, and the psychology of deception can hope to cope with such cleverness.

XI

PSYCHIC PHOTOGRAPHS

Despite the amount of fraud which enters into this subject of so-called spirit photography, I am nevertheless convinced that there are cases of genuine phenomena—in which strange and abnormal markings appear upon photographic plates when no such markings should be present. Amateurs of complete sincerity, who were nevertheless expert photographers, have obtained such results, many of which I myself have seen. Faulty development does not account for these results, nor were the plates light-struck.

In one case I saw, two spirit extras appear upon the plate—remarkably clear, and recognized by many who knew the men in life. Skeptical amateurs took the pictures with a camera and film provided them. No other camera or film was aboard the vessel on which the picture was taken, so that no substitution was possible.

Camera and film remained in the custody of the Captain of the vessel until she docked, when they were immediately turned over to the officials of the company, and by them sent directly to the New York office, where the film was developed by a commercial photographer.

The phantom faces were seen by a number of the crew for many days before the photographs were taken. Their accounts invariably tallied. When photographs of these faces were taken, they appeared upon the film in the spot corresponding to that where they had been seen.

A brief account of the incident first appeared in

Fortune magazine; but a more detailed version was published in the house organ of the Cities Service Company, in February, 1934. This account reads as follows:

CAMERA CATCHES TANKER GHOSTS
Spectral Visitors Seen Daily When SS Watertown *Is in Pacific*

Many strange tales have been woven about the mystery of the sea, but few are more eerie than the story of the Cities Service Tanker, the *SS Watertown*. According to the members of her crew, the ghosts of two of their former shipmates were daily visitors to the ship whenever it ventured into the Pacific Ocean. Following is the story of the men on the *Watertown*.

One day, about five years ago, while the Cities Service Tanker, *Watertown*, was slowly pounding its way through the blue waves of the Pacific, Seamen Courtney and Meehan were assigned to the task of cleaning a cargo tank. While working they were overcome by gas fumes and died before help was forthcoming. Following the tradition of the sea their bodies were lowered into the ocean.

Just before dusk on the following day the entire ship was thrown into an uproar when the heads of the two seamen were clearly distinguished between the second and third stanchions on the catwalk. The ghosts thereupon became the chief topic of conversation in both officers' and seamen's quarters.

This phenomenon occurred daily thereafter, and even the skeptics were being impressed. However, someone suggested taking a photograph of the ghosts, since cameras are not supposed to lie. Accordingly, a camera was obtained and a snapshot taken. With the film intact, the camera was given to the Captain for safekeeping.

The ghosts were daily visitors at the spot where the bodies of the two seamen had been put overboard until the day the ship left the Pacific and entered the Atlantic Ocean. On reaching port, the film was developed and printed, and the stoutest skeptic was convinced—there on the photo were the heads of seamen Courtney and Meehan!

This account is partly inaccurate and partly in accordance with the facts. The men died and were buried at sea; that is a matter of record. It seems also undisputed that practically all the officers and men on deck saw the phantom heads on several occasions. Several were reported to have seen them at the same time. They invariably appeared on the same side of the vessel (the side from which they had been buried) and appeared to follow the ship at the same distance—about one thousand feet. They appeared here and there amid the waves. No official record of all this was made, and no camera was aboard the boat during this voyage.

When the boat docked, the Captain reported the case to the officials of the company, in New Orleans. The first mate procured a camera, and an official of the company supplied a roll of film, which he placed (still sealed) in the Captain's hands just before sailing on the return trip, with instructions to photograph the ghost, if possible. This film was inserted into the camera by the Captain, and the pictures were taken by him.

When the phantom heads were again seen, six exposures were made, and five of these showed nothing unusual. The sixth, however, showed a positive result. The heads were seen only in the Pacific, and always on the same side of the vessel.

After the films had been exposed, the camera remained in the Captain's possession until the boat again docked in New Orleans. The film was then delivered in person by the Captain to Mr. James Patton, an officer of the company, who took it with him to New York, where it was developed by a commercial photographer.

Mr. Patton has since died, and the name of the photographer is at present unknown to any member of the firm. The first mate has since been drowned, and the majority of the crew lost sight of since 1925, when the above occurred.

The Cities Service Company, it should be stated, is a large and reputable corporation, with a suite of offices located at 70 Pine Street, New York. An enlarged photograph of the picture was for some time on exhibition in the lobby of the building in question.

The manager of the New York office of the company, Mr. Storey, very kindly granted me an interview on December 7, 1934, at which time he confirmed the above account, and replied to a number of questions. These, together with his answers, follow:

Q. To whom did the camera belong?
A. The first mate.
Q. Whose idea was it to take the pictures?
A. Mr. J. S. Patton, an officer of the company, now deceased.
Q. Who developed the films?
A. A commercial photographer in New York. I am sorry I cannot give you the name; but he had no connection with the films.
Q. Is there any written record in the files of the company?
A. No official record; it was generally discussed, however, and no explanation of the case was ever found.
Q. Are any of the crew now available, for first-hand testimony?
A. I'm afraid not; the crews were constantly changed, and we have no record of the men after leaving our employ.
Q. What was the reaction of the crew to the specters?
A. So far as I know, all of them who saw them believed in their reality. The skeptics were all below deck!

Q. Why did the Captain of the boat resign?
A. To obtain a better berth elsewhere. He was under no cloud.
Q. Were there any hard feelings about this?
A. No.
Q. Any hard feelings anywhere about the case?
A. None that I know of.
Q. Where is the *Watertown* now?
A. She is due in New York on the 18th of this month.
Q. Did the heads appear constantly or only occasionally?
A. Occasionally.
Q. Did the heads appear by night or only by day?
A. It would be impossible to answer that.
Q. How long were the heads seen?
A. For a few seconds as a rule.
Q. Did the faces register varied expressions?
A. It was probably impossible to determine that.
Q. Did the heads move about as well as keeping up with the ship?
A. They seemed to follow the vessel, but always at the same distance.
Q. Did the heads always look the same?
A. Yes.
Q. Were the heads always the same size?
A. Yes; they appeared to be somewhat larger than in life.
Q. Was there, in your opinion, any possible motive for trickery?
A. No.
Q. Have you had any reason to suspect trickery or practical joking since then?
A. No.
Q. What is your opinion of the photograph?
A. So far as I know, it has never been explained; that's as far as I can go.

Mr. Storey explained that the man with the bald head was Meehan, while the other, James T. Courtney, had been known to the crew as Sunny Jim. The latter's head is said to appear between the stanchions, and is not nearly as clear as that of Meehan, which is remarkably clear and life-like.

It is of course regrettable that the facts did not come to our attention in 1925, when they were still fresh in the minds of the officers and crew, and when practically all of them were available for personal interviews. However, the fact that more than eight years elapsed before the first account appeared in print seems to indicate that there was no desire on the part of the company for publicity. This finally came, I understand, rather accidentally, and with no premeditation on their part.

The above are the facts of this extraordinary case, so far as they can now be verified. There can be no doubt that at least one of the faces is a realistic portrait of the dead man; and that both were repeatedly seen, according to all reports, by various members of the crew, including the officers and Captain.

The writer has no theory to offer of this remarkable case, and the reader is in as good a position as anyone to estimate its validity.

A second instance of spirit photography may be summarized far more briefly. The person who took the photograph has been a personal friend of the author's for many years, and he feels absolutely assured of her honesty and sincerity. She is a good amateur photographer and trained to some extent in the methods and technique of psychical research. Summarized, the case is as follows:

On July 4th she visited some friends in the country, and while there took a snapshot of the house from the lawn. When the photograph was developed there appeared (in the lower left-hand corner) the dim outline of a spirit child, apparently running across the lawn, her

```
*********************************
PAGE (MUSICD1)        DATE DUE: 08/24/88    295-64-0273
S.133CZ35W
Carrington, Hereward, 1880-1959.    C=001    OHI
The world of psychic research.    2306582    MAIL
---------------
IMPORTANT: You are responsible for this    KATHLEEN ELIZABETH DEVAULT
item until it is returned and discharged at    SEND CARE OF
    STATE LIBRARY OF OHIO                    OSU MAIN LIBRARY
    1114 OHIO DEPARTMENTS BLDG.              CIRCULATION DEPT
    65 S. FRONT STREET
*********************************
```

hair and skirts flying. No child was seen by anyone at the time, and no child lived in the immediate neighborhood. The result was of course wholly unexpected.

In order to check her findings, Mrs. B. visited these friends the following weekend, and again photographed the house from the same spot, in order to see if some trick light-effect might perhaps have been responsible. On this second occasion, however, nothing abnormal was noted; nor has any such effect been noted in subsequent photographs.

In thought-photography no camera is used; the plates (or films), wrapped in opaque black paper, are held one at a time against the psychic's forehead, and he is requested to think or concentrate upon a certain mental object or image. After doing so the plate is removed and another one handed him and the operation repeated. The plates and wrappers are numbered, and a list made of the images concentrated upon, so that the accuracy of correspondence may be checked at the end of the demonstration.

The young psychic undertaking these tests is not a medium, but an amateur investigator, with scientific training. The conditions of the experiment rendered fraud impossible. The plates were bought by myself from a reputable photographic supply house (Murphy) and were wrapped by Mr. Burton, of that firm, in opaque black paper in their own darkroom. They were carefully sealed. The wrapped and numbered plates were then delivered to me, and I took them to the sitting in my pocket. They were handed to the psychic one at a time, and he held them against his forehead (in the dim light) while concentrating upon the chosen image. (This was only given him *after* he had held the plate against his forehead.)

At the conclusion of the period of concentration (usually about twelve minutes) the plate was handed to me, and I placed it aside. The next day the unopened packages of plates were turned over to the photographer, who developed them. The only contact permitted was when the medium held the wrapped plates to his forehead.

On theory, there should be no markings upon the plates at all; as a matter of fact some very curious effects were obtained. At first glance one would be tempted to say that these plates were either light-struck or faultily developed. But the sealed wrappings were completely light-proof; while the fact that Murphy's have developed tens of thousands of plates, for their customers, without ever encountering similar effects in any single instance, is surely proof that faulty development cannot be the answer either. Again we are left with a problem on our hands!

One other curious factor should be noted, in connection with this series of psychic photographs. At the request of the psychic, the plates were developed twice the length of time usually necessary for normal exposures. Despite this enormous over-development, the plates came up quite normally, and were not spoiled thereby, as one might have expected. Over-exposure and over-development are two curious features which have often been noted in psychic photography. Here is a suggestive fact, it seems to me, which experimenters in this field should take into account and study in the future—when once the reality of psychic photographs has been established.

XII

THE VISIONS AND VOICES OF JEANNE D'ARC

JEANNE D'ARC—that most magnificent and beautiful figure! Color only, not words, can express her as she was. Her natural wit and patriotism, her keen knowledge of strategy and tactics, her grasp of situations and of the psychological intricacies of character, are all overshadowed and rendered doubly subtle and significant by the extraordinary nature of the motives which lay behind her and prompted her on to greater deeds, to higher and nobler actions. Jeanne did not leave her quiet country home and enter the lists to fight the English simply because of her sense of patriotism; she was not burned at the stake because she successfully conquered the invader; she was not executed because she was irreligious or a heretic; but she suffered death and she achieved all that she did achieve because there was an impelling force behind her, stronger than her own, constantly urging her on and inciting her to action. I do not mean by this that any Divine Providence was directly concerned. Jeanne was devout, to be sure; but that in which she trusted, which spurred her on, and which was the direct cause of her greatness, was the inspiration she received from her visions and voices.

The character of these preternatural visitations is too well known to need restatement in this place. Suffice it to say that Jeanne had implicit faith in the objective or external nature of the voices and of the visions that came to her—warning her when she was in danger, admonishing her to follow this or that course of action, offering her spiritual or material advice, which (so the Maid always maintained) was invariably true and never deceived her. It was because she clung to her belief in the reality of these voices that she was executed as a traitor and a heretic; because of her insistent belief in the supernatural intervention of a higher power in her affairs was she enabled to do as she did, to conquer as she conquered, to be, in short, the historic personage, half saint, half woman, extraordinary genius, that she was.

Needless to say, these visions and voices of Jeanne D'Arc have been attributed to the delusions of a deranged and distorted brain. Present-day materialistic science sees in these visitations naught beyond the hallucinations conjured up by an overwrought and imaginative mind—induced in the first place by excessive fasting and meditation, and objectified until they seemed outstanding realities. Many such cases, it is asserted, may be found in the Salpêtrière, and in many of the hospitals for the nervously and mentally deranged. An overcredulous mind, an emaciated body, a superstitious faith, and much can be accounted for! Thus reasons materialistic psychology; and this is the view of the case which the average reader is inclined to take.

Yet there are numerous strong reasons for thinking that such an analysis of the case fails to cover all the facts. In the first place, Jeanne was not weak in body, nor was her health undermined in her youth when she first saw the visions and heard the voices, nor at any subsequent period of her life, with the exception, perhaps, of those occasions when Jeanne had received wounds of a more or less serious nature, or after her leap from the *donjon* of Beurevoir. One never hears of her ill-health;

on the contrary, all existent reports seem to indicate a remarkable soundness of body and a vigor unsurpassed by any of her soldiers. From the physical point of view, then, we can hardly suppose that Jeanne was likely to suffer from hallucinations such as those commonly seen by the ill or by the insane.

Nor was her mental health more unsound or less vigorous than her bodily vitality. A genius she certainly was; but as genius has been considered dangerously near to insanity, perhaps that goes for little. Sanity, however, may be defined as "the ability to cope with the conditions of everyday life." If that be accepted as just, it can only be said that Jeanne possessed that capacity far more strongly and to a far higher degree than the majority of us can hope for. Her attitude at all times was dignified and courageous; her aims the noblest and best. At no time in her life did she exhibit the faintest indications of her inability to cope with her surroundings and mold the affairs of church and state as only one could mold them who was actuated by the highest, the purest, the most unselfish and sanest of motives.

It is possible, of course, that Jeanne's subconscious mind did play a large part in the creation of these images and in the construction of her voices; but there must have been something more in them than mere hallucination. Like Socrates, the Maid never for a moment wavered in her fixed belief that the intelligences that spoke to her were objective and beyond herself; never did she find them false or misleading or injurious in character; never did they betray her or give her advice contrary to her own welfare or that of the country and the king so precious to her.

And this brings me to the main theme of my sketch. The *character* of internal voices such as those heard by

Jeanne D'Arc must be judged at least partly on their own merits and for what they are worth, so to speak. If these voices had been wicked and misleading and mischievous—if they had deceived the Maid and given her advice contrary to her own good, and to the good of her country—if (which is still more probable) they had been merely dreamlike and incoherent—we should be somewhat justified in thinking that these voices represented nothing more than the results of a disordered mind. But when we find—as we do—that these voices were invariably truth-telling or veridical, as they have been termed, we are certainly justified in thinking that such visitations might be instigated, at least in part, by some intelligence other than that of the Maid; that the voices were real premonitory warnings and indications of guidance received from minds beyond that of Jeanne herself—minds more powerful and far-seeing, who found it possible to use her brain and her organism to express and convey to the world thoughts and sentiments greater than her own; to convey messages of faith, hope and counsel to those capable of acting upon them; and to infuse the energy and life necessary to set into execution the guidance thus conveyed.

It may be, as Mr. Andrew Lang maintained, that "persons entirely sane may be so constituted as to see and hear, as if externally, their ideas and mental impressions"; but that does not explain all the facts, as he himself frankly admits. "Come to the Salpêtrière," said a man of science to an Abbé, "and I'll show you twenty Jeanne D'Arcs!" "Has one of them given us back Alsace and Lorraine?" asked the Abbé. "There is the crux!"

The very fact that the visions and voices of Jeanne were invariably helpful and never harmful, and never inane, lends great weight to the belief that these represented, not the mere objectified hallucinations of a disordered mind, but the results of a clarified vision, which was enabled to perceive and record impressions and messages sent from a sphere of life and intelligence above or beyond our own. And this, I think, has to be granted no matter whether we conceive Jeanne's voices as coming directly from spirits of a higher order, or as representing merely the extreme and vastly extended powers of her own mind—that part of the Self which is enabled, on occasion, to reach out into a world of thought and action, and gather inspiration and light and spiritual illumination, just as we receive material energy by conforming to the highest code of laws of the material plane, and by imbibing as large a draught as possible of the cosmic energy.

XIII

THE PROBLEM OF THE MIND-BODY RELATION

I SHALL BEGIN BY ASKING the reader to grant for our immediate purposes and for the sake of argument that the testimony afforded by our senses and by common sense is correct, that a material world actually exists—composed in the ultimate analysis of atoms and electrons. Our body and brain are likewise material. They occupy space and have weight. The brain is the organ of thought. Certain chemical, physical and electrical changes take place in the brain whenever we think, and our thoughts are somehow connected with these changes. The mind, on the other hand, seems to be immaterial; it occupies no space, has no weight, cannot be discovered by means of anatomical dissection, and so forth. When a man dies he is thought to be no lighter than before. Inner observation nevertheless proves to us that mental activity is *real*. It is our very Self.

Assuming for our present purposes that this is true, we have thus a material entity (the brain), actively functioning, and an immaterial entity (the mind), also actively functioning. Somehow these two are associated or connected one with another. How? We must now briefly review the answers to this question which have been advanced by philosophers in the past.

The first theory to be discussed is what may be called automatism. This contends that there is only one definite chain of causation—the physical. Each successive brain-

PROBLEM OF THE MIND-BODY

change is conditioned and determined by the one preceding it. We have here a chain of physical events—the brain-changes. Corresponding with these are our thoughts, constituting the flow of consciousness. These thoughts are not causally connected one with another. They are merely resultant from the brain-changes, which are the fundamental things. Just as the shadow of a horse accompanies the horse, in somewhat the same manner our thoughts accompany the physiological changes within the brain. They are the mere resultant of the brain's activity. (This is of course a materialistic conception.) Let us now examine this theory very briefly, and see some of the difficulties involved in accepting it.

In the first place, it has been pointed out that this theory involves a distinct breach of continuity, from the point of view of biology. The appearance of consciousness at some undefined point in the course of the evolution of the animal kingdom, as postulated by it, constitutes this break. Something new (consciousness or mind) appears, without any reason for its doing so.

In the second place, this idea runs counter to the law of conservation of energy, and even the law of causality, for in all other cases the cause passes over into the effect, and, in a physical process of any kind, if the cause is physical the effect must be physical also. But in this case the cause appears to be physical and the event nonphysical, for the brain-change is a physical event, while the resultant sensation or thought is not. We can conceive of a brain-change producing another brain-change, but not a thought, and at this point the law of causation seems to be violated.

Finally, it has been pointed out that the shadow (thought) seems to be the important thing in this case, rather than the horse (brain event), for we can conceive of a horse causing a shadow, but not of a shadow producing a horse! Yet the thought seems to be the vital and essential thing for us, and indeed constitutes the very core of our mental being. For all these reasons, therefore, this theory of epiphenomenalism, as it has been called, has been largely given up, and is today held by few if any philosophers of front-rank importance.

The next theory which may be mentioned is idealism, which contends that thought is the only reality, and that what we perceive as brain-changes are really mental in their ultimate analysis—being but the expression of thought on the physical plane. Apart from its challenge to common sense, it will be observed that this view is just as difficult of acceptance as the other; for, if it be impossible for us to conceive how brain-changes can produce consciousness, it is equally difficult for us to understand how thoughts can produce brain-changes. The problem is the same in either case. We may therefore dismiss this theory also.

Next, we have the doctrine of psycho-physical parallelism, which holds that brain-changes and thoughts run along side by side, so to say, without ever influencing one another. They merely co-exist or are coincidental in point of time, but there is no real causal connection between them. Although this doctrine is held by not a few philosophers, it seems erroneous on the face of it, and opposed to the experience of everyday life, for we know that bodily changes can affect mental changes and vice versa. As Professor William James said: "It is quite inconceivable that consciousness should have *nothing to do* with a business which it so faithfully attends." We may therefore dismiss this theory as not logical nor reasonable.

Phenomenalistic Parallelism. This is the theory maintained by Kant, Spinoza and others. It holds that both brain and consciousness (or body and mind) are but two different expressions of one underlying reality—just as the convex and concave surfaces of a sphere are but two expressions of an underlying reality. As to the nature of this reality, Kant and Herbert Spencer were content to call it X, or the unknown, while Spinoza maintained that it was God.

It would be impossible, in our brief space, to discuss the various pros and cons of this theory; suffice it to say that Prof. McDougall and other psychologists reject it, and that Prof. Stumpf says of it: "The one substance which is supposed to manifest itself in the two attributes, the physical and the psychical, is nothing but a word which expresses the desire to escape from dualism, but which does not really bridge the gulf for our understanding."

Two other theories may be mentioned, in passing, merely to include them. The first of these is known as solipsism, which maintains that nothing really exists outside the perceiving consciousness. This is palpably ridiculous, inasmuch as other minds have as great a right to their existence as has ours.

The second is crude materialism, which maintains that matter and energy are the only realities, and that mind and thought do not actually exist at all, except as a by-product of matter in motion or energy. This view is nowhere maintained by psychologists or philosophers today. Matter *per se* cannot think. As Huxley said, in writing of this view: "All this I heartily disbelieve. In the first place it seems to me pretty plain that there is a third thing in the universe, to wit, consciousness, which, in the hardness of my heart or head, I cannot see to be matter or force, or any conceivable modification of either, however intimately the manifestations of consciousness may be connected with the phenomena known as matter or force...."

Thought has a definite *meaning,* and therein consists the stumbling-block. Both matter and force are blind. Neither of them has any meaning, while thought has. Thought, therefore, if a mere manifestation of energy, must be energy-plus-X (the meaning of the thought), and in the X we encounter the difficulty! It is that which differentiates thought from matter and energy as we know them. This is our problem, and to ignore it is not to solve it.

Other Theories

We may now consider very briefly one or two other views which have been advanced in the past, regarding this difficult mind-body problem, though they are really subdivisions of one or other of the theories mentioned above. The first of these is the view elaborated by Prof. W. K. Clifford, known as the mind stuff theory. This contends that "mind stuff is the reality which we perceive as matter. A moving molecule of inorganic matter does not possess mind or consciousness, but it possesses a small piece of mind stuff. When the molecules are so combined together as to form the film on the underside of a jellyfish, the elements of mind stuff which go along with them are so combined as to form the faint beginnings of sentience. When the molecules are so combined as to form the brain and nervous system of a vertebrate, the corresponding elements of mind stuff are so combined as to form some kind of consciousness. When matter takes the complex form of a living human brain, the corresponding mind stuff takes the form of a human consciousness having intelligence and volition."

PROBLEM OF THE MIND-BODY 145

This mosaic theory of consciousness, however, has many difficulties, one of the most fundamental being that it fails to explain the antithesis between subject and object. Further, mind is not a static thing, but is active and dynamic, changing and creating. Tiles may be placed together so as to form a certain pattern, it is true, but the produced pattern *does* nothing. For these reasons, therefore—and others which it would take us too long to enumerate here—we must conclude that this theory is anything but satisfactory as an explanation of consciousness.

Prof. Percival Lowell, in his *Occult Japan,* advances the following theory as to the nature of mind: "The only logical explanation of matter and mind is that the *two are one;* and that the life-principle of the whole is some mode of motion. When we have, as we say, an 'idea,' what happens inside us is probably something like this: the neural current of molecular change passes up the nerves, and through the ganglia reaches at last the cortical cells and excites a change there. Now the nerve cells have been so often thrown into this particular form of wave-motion that they vibrate with great ease. The nerves, in short, are good conductors, and the current passes swiftly along them, but when it reaches the cortical cells, it finds a set of molecules which are not so accustomed to this special change. The current encounters resistance, and in overcoming this resistance it causes the cells to glow. This white-heating of the cells we call consciousness. Consciousness, in short, is probably nerve-glow."

This theory has at least one advantage over some of the others before mentioned: it makes consciousness dynamic instead of static; a *go* instead of a *thing.* However, there are certain fundamental difficulties in this theory, which prevent its acceptance.

In the first place, sensations are not the only realities. Thinking originates within us. In the second place, we have every right to assume that nervous currents which are carried along by other nerves would meet with no greater resistance within the brain than outside it. Thirdly, we have the fatal objection that this theory, again, fails to take into account the most fundamental part of all thought—as before mentioned—meaning. No amount of nerve-glow can solve one of Euclid's problems. The creative side of consciousness, the meaning of all thought, is totally neglected on this view; yet for us this is the most important and central factor, constituting in short our very Self as we know it.

Interactionism or Animism

There remains one view of this problem which we have so far not considered. This is the theory which our common sense and inner feelings tell us is the true one; namely, that mind and brain appear to be two separate and distinct things, which interact and influence one another. In sensation, the mind is affected through the brain. In volition, the body is affected by the mind. Both entities exist in their own worlds, and are merely associated together in some mysterious fashion. It is of course a dualistic theory. Mix poison in a man's blood, and it will eventually reach his brain and eclipse consciousness. Here we have the action of the body on the mind. Think and feel strongly enough within yourself, and the body will be affected in turn, even to the point of causing death. Here we have the action of the mind on the body. We inwardly feel that something of the sort takes place.

Of course, two grave objections to this view are (a) that it is frankly dualistic, and (b) that the *how* of the connection and mutual influences remains largely unexplained.

PROBLEM OF THE MIND-BODY

Nevertheless, this view has appealed to many thinkers and is, as we know, the one to which Prof. William McDougall was driven at the end of his lengthy book, *Body and Mind*.

As the result of this discussion, then, it may be said that no particular theory as to the relation of brain and mind can be held to be definitely accepted, or free from certain fundamental objections. Some psychologists and philosophers favor one view, some another. From the point of view of common experience and common sense, interactionism seems plausible, but involves a dualistic scheme of things, which is objectionable to many. It may be pointed out, however, that it is intrinsically no more dualistic than psycho-physical parallelism, which also postulates the mind as a distinct and separate entity. Yet this doctrine has been accepted by many skeptical thinkers.

My own point of view is that this question can only be settled by an actual appeal to *fact,* and that philosophical theories will have to follow demonstration. If the advances of modern science—and particularly psychic science—ultimately prove that *mind can exist and function independent of a physical brain,* then these metaphysical theories will have to be remolded in accordance with the facts. It remains for the science of the future to settle this question one way or the other.

Science deals with facts, and to a certain extent with the interpretation of those facts. When this explanatory process reaches a certain point, however, we arrive at the threshold of metaphysics. All final or ultimate explanations must be couched largely in these terms. The majority of scientific men refuse to "go the whole way," being content with more or less pragmatic explanations, leaving severely alone all attempts at ultimate explanations. Nevertheless, such ultimates are needed, if we wish to arrive at any satisfactory understanding of the universe about us. Until the past generation, philosophers divorced themselves from science; now the two proceed more or less hand-in-hand, and there is every indication that this happy inter-blending will continue. Metaphysicians are becoming more scientific, and scientists are becoming more metaphysical.

Present-day science, however, is still largely mechanistic in its viewpoint. It is based upon the more or less tacit assumption that mystical and psychic experiences of all kinds are necessarily *illusory*.

If, however, such phenomena actually exist—if supernormal manifestations really occur—then both science and philosophy will have to be expanded so as to include them, and find a place for them in some larger cosmos. They must influence both fundamentally. A new body of facts will have to be incorporated into science, and philosophy will have to expand its explanatory hypotheses in order to cover and include them. Significant changes will be necessitated. A whole new system will have to be built up, based upon the validity of these newer facts, and psychical research will thus become the most influential and important of all human activities (instead of the "Cinderella of the Sciences") by showing us that life and mind are as real as matter and motion, and that the human spirit is, after all, worthy of a dignified and respected place in the scheme of human thought.

Psychic science alone can do this, and is doubtless destined in the near future to rule and dominate the whole world of thought, and to influence the belief of humanity as to its ultimate destiny and the meaning of life!

XIV

FREE WILL AND DETERMINISM IN THE LIGHT OF PSYCHIC PHENOMENA

THERE IS NO PROBLEM in the whole history of philosophy which has vexed the minds of men more than that of free will—whether the will of man is free (as it seems to be to the person willing) or whether it is governed by strict laws and determined by prior causal factors, in which case the inner feeling of freedom which we experience is illusory. Hundreds of volumes have been written upon this subject; but it is possible that, even so, some new light may be thrown upon it by psychic phenomena once their actuality be established.

First, let us define our terms. From the popular or common sense point of view everyone knows very well what is meant by free will. It means that the individual is free to perform any action or make any decision he pleases. If he goes out of the front door he feels free to turn to the right or to the left, whichever he decides, and he can will to turn and walk in either direction. The fiat of the will is thought in this view to initiate and carry out the decision. Man is free at any moment to do anything he pleases!

But a moment's reflection will show us that the problem is not so simple as this. In the first place a man can will until he is black in the face to jump from New York to London but he will never be able to do it. Space and certain mechanical restrictions prevent him from doing so.

Man therefore must have only a *limited* freedom. How limited, and by what?

The analogy of the chess board has often been used. Every piece on the board is limited to certain moves; a pawn can move only one square at a time (after the initial move) and must "take" diagonally; the bishop can move only diagonally and the rook vertically or horizontally, and so on. Nevertheless, subject to these limitations, the combined moves and relationships of the chessmen can become highly complicated and divergent as the game of chess shows us. These varying combinations are brought about not by the chessmen themselves but by the mind of the player manipulating them. *His* is the directive mentality at work. Although each individual move is conditioned, therefore, the combined pattern formed by the men is not. The directive mentality or free will of the player is responsible for this.

So, it has been suggested, although individual actions in our lives are determined and limited, nevertheless, the pattern of life may be decided by the mind and will of the person living it.

But just what do we mean by will? Here we encounter another highly controversial topic. Modern psychology does not recognize the existence of will in the older meaning of that term. It contends that the act of willing consists merely in a choice between two or more alternatives. Confronted with two alternatives, a choice between them must be made; and this act of choosing constitutes the essence of willing. The feeling of willing is merely this choice between alternative actions or decisions. On this view there is no longer any such thing as will. It is an illusion. (In all the above, and in what follows, it must be understood that I am merely attempting to express in very

FREE WILL AND DETERMINISM 151

simple and popular language highly technical, psychological and metaphysical principles.)

It will be observed that, in both these conclusions, modern science runs counter to our inner feelings and the point of view of common sense. We all *feel* that we are free, and we *feel* that we can exercise or exert will-power. Nevertheless, science says that these feelings are illusory, and that neither of them exist as entities in the world.

The point of view of occult science has of course always been precisely the opposite: it has contended that will and freedom of the will are both factual, and that the human will can actually exercise a dynamic function, when rightly exercised, capable not only of influencing the life of the individual but also affecting minds and even matter beyond the limits of the organism, and of projecting so-called thought-forms. Both theoretical and experimental data are offered in support of these views.

And now what is the view taken by academic science? It is that cause and effect are universally applicable and inescapable. There can be no effect without a cause and vice versa. All events are determined by the chain of preceding causes, so that if one could know *all* there is to be known about a certain cause, one could invariably predict the effect, and there would be no possibility of the effect being otherwise. Results, actions, effects are always determined strictly by the preceding causes.

In the material world this principle seems to work out well enough. An eclipse can be predicted 1,002 years hence. Ever since the time of Newton strict determinism has ruled classical physics. Goethe's "eternal iron laws" were based upon this principle. Nature represented a huge mechanism, a vast machine. Man, as a part of this machine, must belong to it, and the general principle of determinism must rule his life accordingly. Man's thoughts and actions are all subject to this Great Law; all of them are, in the last analysis, *determined*.

Just what are we to understand by this, as applied to man? Perhaps this can best be illustrated by a concrete example. Supposing a man is standing on the edge of a precipice; he decides to jump off and actually does so, committing suicide. Now, the determinists would say this man's decision and action were both strictly determined; he could not possibly have thought and acted otherwise. Furthermore, if we lined up a hundred men on the edge of the same precipice, and every influence in their lives up to that time had been *absolutely* identical, then every one of them would similarly jump off, and none of them could possibly do otherwise. The preceding chain of causes in their lives having been identical, the effect in every instance must be identical also.

This, crudely put, is the doctrine of determinism as applied to man. He is a part of a great machine. Like it, he is strictly determined. It is, of course, a materialistic doctrine, and as such fought tooth and nail by religious teachers who contended that, were this doctrine true, it would do away altogether with the moral order of the world. Man would no longer be responsible to God or even to society for his actions. He could not possibly think, feel and act otherwise than as he does.

This doctrine of determinism has been extended in many directions, leading to the belief in fatalism, predestination, predeterminism, and so forth. These doctrines have greatly influenced the oriental mind. Elaborate attempts have even been made to dovetail these doctrines into the most dogmatic religions.

I have spoken above of the attitude of modern science and classical physics. Within the past few years, however,

FREE WILL AND DETERMINISM 153

great changes have come about in this realm. Heisenberg's "uncertainty principle" served as a rude shock to the smugly entrenched world of academic physicists. For this showed that strict determinism was seemingly impossible even within the physical world. It showed that the future could never be foretold with exactitude, because the present can never be completely known. Probability was all that could be determined; or as Ernst Zimmer said in *The Revolution in Physics:* "Profounder experience has now taught us that it [determinism] must be replaced by a law of a more general character, which allows us to predict from a state known to us, with a certain degree of uncertainty, what will happen within certain limits in the future."

All this, it will be observed, relates to the world of matter and energy, in which the doctrine of determinism was thought to be most strongly entrenched, and from which it was extended to the world of life and mind. In the latter, determinism was only assumed to exist because of its seeming proof in the physical world and by analogy. It had frequently been pointed out, however, that such proof, as soon as life was introduced into the equation, became far more difficult. As Bergson expressed it: "One can predict an eclipse a thousand years hence, but no one can predict what will happen when you pull a dog's tail!"

No, when life and mind are introduced, it becomes next to impossible to *prove* determinism; while subjective experience and common sense tell us that it does not exist. Man feels, thinks and acts all through life *as if* he had free will—whether he actually has it or not. For all practical purposes, then, man lives as though it were true.

It may now be asked: "What has all this to do with psychical research? And what has psychical research to do with it?" This: In cases of prediction, prophecy, precognition, and so on, the future is seemingly foreseen, sometimes with uncanny accuracy. Even as cautious a critic of the evidence as Mr. H. F. Saltmarsh (in his little book *Foreknowledge*) was compelled to admit that genuine premonitions and predictions exist, and that the veil of the future is sometimes actually lifted. This being so, the question at once arises: "How is this possible, inasmuch as the future does not yet seemingly exist?"

If the doctrine of determinism were true, one could perhaps understand, however dimly, such a phenomenon, since the future would flow as a natural consequence from the present. But then mechanistic determinism would render such forms of psychic phenomena "impossible." If free will were true, on the contrary, there would be plenty of latitude for spirits and a spiritual world; but then the future would be unpredictable, because it would be modified and changed from moment to moment by the mind of the individual. On either view foreseeing of the future should be impossible. Yet it is an undoubted fact. How can we reconcile all this?

In discussing the future, we at once become involved with the concept of *time*. The general idea of time is that it is a sort of stream, flowing along in one dimension. A given point on this line represents the present moment; the line to one side of it would then represent the past, while the line extending in the other direction would represent the future. Our point, however, is not static. It is constantly moving forward into the future at an even pace. It thus represents a sort of knife-edge between two eternities. The past does not exist: it has gone forever. The future does not exist; it has not yet arrived. What then does exist? The present moment. But the present moment can hardly be said to exist either, since it is no sooner here than it is gone. What was the future is now

FREE WILL AND DETERMINISM

present—and is now past! There must be something wrong with this conception of time, inasmuch as it can render such a paradoxical situation possible.

In the first place, has the past really ceased to exist? In one sense no, because if it had, we should have no memory and no history. But we have. Therefore, the past must exist in *some* sense; not as a material reality to be sure, but in some sphere of its own. The past, in short, cannot *not* exist. Similarly, it has been contended, the future may also exist in a certain sense in a sphere of its own, as a sort of matrix into which the present is constantly moving. Were this true, one could begin to have some faint inkling as to how the future might at times be foreseen. But then the future would be apparently fixed or determined—unless it were an *elastic* future. And if it were, the difficulty in perceiving it would be proportional to such elasticity. Even granting this, the central problem would yet remain: How—by what process—is the future ever foreseen at all? How is such supernormal knowledge possible?

Here we arrive at the crux of our problem; the heart of the matter. I shall endeavor to be as brief and explicit as possible in discussing this question.

In the first place, then, there are certain types of premonitions which may be explained by referring them to the normal action of the subconscious mind. Bodily illnesses would fall into this category. Thus, if A. had a vivid dream, in which he saw himself with a skin eruption, and a day or so later actually "broke out" in this manner, one might well be tempted to suppose that his subconscious mind had sensed the inner condition of his body long before the conscious mind, and had used the dream as a means of externalizing this information. In such a case any supernormal theory would not be necessitated.

Let us take two cases of another type. A spider is walking across a table. You say, "I *predict* that when the spider reaches the edge of the table it will fall off," and sure enough it does! Or you meet a friend on the street and say to him, "I *predict* that when you get to the street-corner your hat will be lifted from your head," and it is. In the latter case you knew something about the environment of your friend which he did not, that there was a strong wind blowing down the side street, and that this wind might tear his hat off. Your greater knowledge enabled you to make this prediction.

Similarly, it has been suggested, there may be intelligences possessing greater knowledge than do we of our lives—their trends and tendencies. This knowledge would enable them to make predictions of limited accuracy. The general tenor of the prediction in that case would be: "If you continue your present line of action I can foresee that such-and-such a result will come to pass." If that line of action be followed, the prediction would be accurate; if, on the other hand, it were changed, the prediction would be wrong. The stumbling-block in this theory, of course, is the postulation of such supernormally-gifted external intelligences—which few scientific men would accept!

Then there is the theory of the "eternal now." Briefly stated, this means that the future already exists in some sense—being perceived by us as present, when we come to that point in space and time when we can perceive it as such. An analogy may help to make this clear.

Suppose you are riding on the rear platform of a train which is in motion. You peer to the right and to the left. As the train proceeds, new vistas keep passing into your range of vision; you see mountains, valleys, trees on your right, and meadows, rivers and cottages on your left. As the train continues its progress, these fade into the

FREE WILL AND DETERMINISM 157

distance and are lost to view, being replaced by still other vistas. But the mountains, rivers, trees, and houses existed before you perceived them; and they continue to exist after they have passed from your field of vision. You perceived them as present only when you came to that point in time and space when you could perceive them as present. Similarly, it has been suggested, past and future may likewise co-exist with the present, but are only perceived by us as realities when they are crossed by the present moment.

Those of my readers who saw that charming play, *Berkeley Square,* will remember the picture therein drawn —a man in a boat, rowing down an S-shaped river. Behind him lies a bend which has now passed from his sight; it is his past. Before him, around the next bend, lies a vista which he does not yet perceive; it is his future. But, to a man in an airplane, who can see *both* bends in the river, past, present, and future are all *one;* they exist for him as an "eternal now."

Such a view of the case is of course highly metaphysical, and is hard to reconcile with the point of view of common sense and common experience, which tells us that a man cannot experience an accident and die as the result of it, and yet be alive and viewing himself as alive, and actually *being* alive, at the time!

Other theories have been advanced, which it would take too long to epitomize here: The theory of serialism, advanced by J. W. Dunne, in his books, *An Experiment With Time* and *The Serial Universe;* the theory tentatively advanced by Professors Broad and H. H. Price, of another time at right angles, as it were, to our present time, flowing in one dimension; the theory advanced by Mr. H. F. Saltmarsh, of a timeless subliminal consciousness in which past and present are linked into one whole; as well as several others. It would take us too far afield to consider all these.

One other factor should, however, be mentioned in this connection. It is that the past at times is seemingly cognized supernormally, as well as the future. Mr. Myers suggested the term "retrocognition" for such cases, a number of which are on record. They are not perhaps as intrinsically inconceivable as precognition cases, but they are extremely difficult to account for nevertheless. They have at least this much in common: that, at the moment of their perception by the seer, they constitute at that instant the *present*—just as a recalled memory is, at the moment of its recall, not a past but a present event. This is an interesting point which calls for further psychological elaboration.

There is one additional point of considerable interest which should be mentioned here. It is that of a varied series of potential futures, as presented by W. B. Seabrook in his book *Jungle Ways*. This theory, it should be stated, was advanced by an African witch doctoress named Wamba, and, as she expressed it in her own simple language, it can be paraphrased as follows:

Here you come to a clearing in the jungle. From that clearing there are five paths leading through the jungle. If you choose the first path, a lion may spring upon you and kill you; if you choose the second one, you may come to a cool spring of water; if you choose the third one, you may come upon a friendly tribe of natives who will entertain you. Now, *by no process of reasoning can you tell which path to choose.* At every moment in our lives the future stretches before us, not as a straight line but as a series of choices. The future, in short, is always fan-shaped. Numerous possibilities always loom before us.

We can see that this is true in our daily lives. When

FREE WILL AND DETERMINISM

you go out of your front door, you may turn to the right or to the left, or you may cross the street, or you may decide to turn back and reenter the house. Suppose you turn to the right; at the street corner you may accidentally meet a man or woman whom you may ultimately marry! This would not have happened had you chosen any of the other alternatives. How can one tell which course to pursue? Certainly not through any wisdom imparted by means of the much-vaunted conscious mind. Prompting by some higher mind is necessary. (Believing as they do in the supernormal powers of their witch doctors, it is the most natural thing in the world for the natives to seek such information. The only problem is: How does the witch doctor obtain his information? And here we are back at our same old problem again.)

One might extend this analogy of the fan, of course, indefinitely. From each spoke of our fan might extend other ramifications, like the branches of a tree, and the ability to follow *all* these would be beyond the pale of the imagination, since every one of them would depend upon the preceding branch being the one followed by the individual in question. All of them would remain possibilities, in short, mere *potential* futures, which might or might not be traversed.

There is one further complicating factor in precognition cases which occasionally arises, and, inasmuch as this bears directly upon the question of the free will and determinism, it should be mentioned here.

In certain cases, an accident has been *prevented* from happening because of the supernormal warning previously received. Thus, in one case a lady foresaw an automobile accident in which she was involved, and saw (in the vision) her chauffeur afterward step in a certain direction which resulted in his slipping, and thus another accident. When the automobile smash actually happened some days later, she remembered this incident, and prevented her chauffeur from moving in the direction he had intended.

In this case, it will be observed, the second accident was actually prevented from happening. Yet it *would* have happened, precisely as foreseen, if it had not been prevented. The point to bear in mind here is that the recipient of the vision could not have perceived the future content of her own mind at the time (a fourth dimensional slice as it were) because she foresaw the accident otherwise; nor did she perceive the event exactly as it happened in the future, as it did not occur precisely as seen, part of it being altered by her own quick action. She did not foresee the prevention of the second accident, but the accident itself. What was seen, apparently, was the event as it would have occurred had it not been prevented from occurring! In this case the free will of the recipient of the vision seemed to have played a part.

This whole question of foreseeing the future makes us almost certain that our current conceptions of time are fundamentally erroneous. They must be altered if such facts be true. Philosophers in the past, when discussing the question of time, have completely ignored this possibility. They have proceeded on the tacit assumption that the future is *never* foreseen, and have conducted their arguments accordingly. But if supernormal sensing of the future be a fact—as such premonition cases prove it to be —then their arguments will have to be revised and this possibility included within their purview. It will be interesting to see the intellectual squirmings which will ensue when this necessity is forced upon them!

Free will, determinism, causality, time, and many other metaphysical concepts are therefore involved in such premonition cases. They complicate and at the same time tend to throw light upon such problems. But it is obvious that, were the actuality of genuine premonition cases once recognized, all future discussions of these questions would necessarily be revolutionized. These ridiculed and despised psychic phenomena would then, in short, profoundly influence our philosophy—just as they are ultimately bound to affect our science, and particularly our biological and psychological science—once their reality be granted and their implications realized. That day, many of us feel, is not far off.

XV

YOGA AND MAGIC

It may be of interest to compare, very briefly, certain analogies and parallels which exist between the teachings of Yoga philosophy, on the one hand, and occult and magical traditions on the other. At the same time certain of the lesser-known aspects of Yoga may be stressed as throwing light upon these similarities. First of all, however, a brief outline of the general teaching may be necessary, in order to make clear the fundamentals involved, and certain aspects which are held to be basically essential.

The main object of Yoga is the attainment of cosmic consciousness. The cultivation of psychic phenomena cannot be considered the prime objective—though it is claimed that such phenomena develop spontaneously while these exercises are being followed.

The whole course of Yoga training may be divided into eight parts, consisting of steps or stages in development. The first two of these are Yama and Niyama, and these comprise a thorough cleansing of the body, by means of internal hydrotherapy, diet, and so forth, coupled with a system of mental control, in which detachment from worldly goods and desires is attained. These preliminaries are very essential before anyone begins actual work upon the various Yoga practices.

The third stage is known as Asana, and deals with correct bodily posture. This has for its object, first, the quieting of the physical body, and second, the facilitation

YOGA AND MAGIC

of the circulation within it of certain psychic energies.*

When one begins to meditate, it will be noticed that the first thing that interferes with the flow of thought is the body. One becomes fidgety, and a constant change of position is unconsciously sought. This fact was noted by the early experimenters in this field, who contended that there must be *some* bodily postures that could be assumed, which would prevent the body from interfering with concentration. They accordingly experimented and discovered some eighty-four such postures, any one of which, when assumed, may be maintained for hours at a time without necessitating change and without any intrusion by the body upon the placid flow of thought.

Some of these postures are extremely difficult for the ordinary Westerner to assume, such as the famous Buddha position, in which the legs are crossed, the heels being tucked into the groins on the opposite sides of the body. Some of them, however, are relatively simple, and any one of them may be chosen by the beginner.

The second object of Asana, as we have said, is to facilitate the flow of the psychic energies within the body. This we shall come to later. It is essential, however, that the spine be kept straight, in all these Asana positions.

The fourth step or stage deals with Pranayama, which in western terminology means (primarily) breathing exercises. The Yogis contend that, when we breathe, we take into the lungs not only the chemical constituents of the air, but also a subtle, vital energy known as Prana. This is retained in the body when the breath is held and, by certain mental exercises, it is sent around the body,

---

* It must be understood, in all that follows, that I am attempting merely to give a résumé of the Yoga *teachings,* without criticism on the one hand or endorsement on the other. I am presenting merely a summary of what is *taught.*

and particularly down the spine, to awaken certain psychic centers that are essential to development.

Various complicated breathing exercises are accordingly prescribed, into which we have no time to enter at the moment. The period of time between breaths is gradually lengthened in order to insure a greater intake of Prana, while the breath is held for as long as possible in order to manipulate this Prana, when thus retained in the body. These breathing exercises should of course be undertaken gradually and with extreme caution by the beginner, and it is best to have an instructor when undertaking any form of Pranayama.

Associated with this stage is another form of breath control (or rather utilization) known as Mantrayoga, which deals with Mantras or chants. These consist in the constant repetition of certain words or combinations of words, the vibrations of which are said to stimulate the inner psychic faculties.

One of the most famous of these Mantras is the word Om, or more properly Aum. This word enters into nearly all Mantras, and is thought to have a peculiar and unique significance.

Perhaps the most famous of all the oriental Mantras is "Aum Mani Padme Hum," which, roughly translated, means, "O the Jewel in the Lotus." However, the meaning of any particular Mantrum is not the significant factor; it is the actual sound of the word or phrase itself which is important.

Regarding this sacred Mantrum Aum there is much which might be said. It has exoteric, esoteric and mystical meanings. The A is formed in the throat, the U at the roof of the mouth, and the M by the lips. This triplicity also stands for Brahma, Vishnu and Shiva. Its vibrations are said to have "built the worlds," while all sounds are

YOGA AND MAGIC

contained within it. Properly uttered, it is said to influence animals and birds, who respond to and apprehend in part its inner significance.

Now a word as to the famous "Aum Mani Padme Hum." Analyzed more in detail its syllables have been tabulated as follows:

AUM	White	Connected with the gods
MA	Blue	Connected with non-gods
NI	Yellow	Connected with men
PAD	Green	Connected with animals
ME	Red	Connected with non-men
HUM	Black	Connected with dwellers in the purgatories

These six syllables constitute a chain of in-and-out breathing, like a rubber band which is never broken. The analogy has been used of a huge, elongated figure-eight, which emerges from and returns to the mouth.

The interpretation of the Mantum, "O the Jewel in the Lotus," has various symbolical meanings. The Lotus is the world, and the Jewel within it the Buddha's teachings. Or, the Lotus is the mind, and the Jewel within it knowledge; and so on.

In the fifth stage or step we come to the mind and its inner development. It is known as Pratyahara, and means meditation. The Yogis contend that, if you wish to write anything upon a blackboard, the blackboard must be clean; if you wish to write upon the sand, the sand must be free from hillocks and undisturbed by wind or water. Similarly, before you can begin to do anything with the mind, it must be stilled or quieted; and this is accomplished, first, by shutting off external stimuli entering through the senses, and second, by internal quieting mental processes.

In order to close the senses a quiet, secluded spot is

sought, and the eyes, ears and nostrils are closed with the fingers of the hands (of course during Pranayama). The internal stilling processes are more complicated, but may be summarized in a few words as follows:

If you turn your attention inwards you will find that your mind is a most restless and unruly member. It turns and twists like a sea serpent, and does not remain still for an instant. Various visualizing exercises are consequently given in order to still the mind—such as imagining a bucket of water, the contents of which are swishing back and forth, and the water (of the mind) must gradually be calmed down until the agitation is stilled.

After the mind has been thus controlled, we pass on to the sixth step, known as Dharana, which means concentration. After the mind has been quieted we begin to *do* something with it. Various exercises in concentration are accordingly undertaken. These consist for the most part in mental images held before the mind, without allowing the mind to waver or wander from the object of contemplation.

Take for example a Maltese cross. The mental image of this is held firmly before the mind, and it will be found that, while doing so, the cross tends to undergo all sorts of changes or variations. It will change its shape or color, or perhaps disappear altogether. All these wanderings of the mind, from the object of contemplation, are technically known as "breaks," that is, breaks in consciousness. The number of these breaks in any given period of concentration should be carefully noted. A simple means of testing the number of breaks is by pulling over a bead on a string—separating it from a number of beads which have been threaded upon it. The number of beads pulled over will afterward indicate the number of breaks. (This is, of course, the origin of the Christian

YOGA AND MAGIC

practice of "telling the beads," existent many hundreds of years B.C.)

In the seventh stage, known as Dhyana, we come to a process of unification, which is difficult to explain in a few words.

When you are looking at an object, you are conscious of at least two things, namely, the object and yourself. This, the Yogis say, is an illusion, and is due to the fatal duality of the human mind; that is, its faulty, intrinsic structure. In reality there is, they say, only *one* reality in the universe, namely, the absolute consciousness, and if there is an appearance of twoness, or duality, this is an illusion—one of the varied forms of Maya. It must be realized that there is but one absolute thing in the universe, the all-pervading consciousness, of which we are but individual expressions or "rays." When this has been realized the seventh stage has been mastered.

In the eighth step, Samadhi, this unification with the absolute consciousness is achieved. A sort of "click" takes place in the mind, and you and the object of contemplation are no longer two, but one. You are part of the absolute consciousness, and become one with it. In this way cosmic consciousness, or liberation, is ultimately attained.

During this process of development, however, various psychic powers have automatically been acquired. The Yogi does not seek to develop telepathy, clairvoyance, and so on, but claims that these powers will come spontaneously during the course of training. There is, however, a very special reason why this development should take place, which, according to the Yogis, depends upon what seems to us a wholly mythical system of physiology.

It is their contention that there are, within the human body, seven primary psychic centers known as Lotuses or

Chakras. These in the ordinary individual are quiescent; but when stimulated into activity constitute the basis of all psychic power.

Such Chakras or centers are situated in various parts of the body and, as we have said, have been symbolically referred to as Lotuses, because they are said to possess a certain number of petals, and upon these petals various Sanskrit letters are written. They are also variously colored. There are not, of course, any actual letters upon the petals, because there are no actual petals either. They represent, rather, vital foci or centers of psychic energy. Hence, when the body is dissected, these centers are not found, since they are not composed of physical matter but are etheric in character.

The lowest of these centers is said to reside at the base of the spine; the second at the root of the sexual organ; the third is near the solar plexus; the fourth near the heart; the fifth is in the throat; the sixth between the eyebrows, while the seventh is above the head—showing the extent to which their physiology differs from ours. This seventh center is thought to reside within the aura, or magnetic atmosphere, surrounding the human body.

Now, in the lowest of these centers, there is said to reside a powerful, subtle energy known as the Kundalini, which is usually symbolized by a serpent, having three and a half coils, with its head erected like a cobra. As this energy is stimulated into activity it arouses each in turn the seven Chakras, or vital centers in the body, activating them and causing them to become dynamic instead of static. It is upon the arousing of this energy that psychic phenomena depend. The question is: How is it aroused?

In order to explain this, we must return to the beginning of our study. The proper Asana (position), with spine erect, facilitates the passage of the psychic energies

YOGA AND MAGIC

through the body, and particularly through the spine, down the center of which a hollow tube is thought to exist, known as the Sushumna. In Pranayama the Prana is taken into the lungs, whence it is circulated or propelled, by an effort of will, down this hollow tube in the spine against the lowest of the psychic centers. This finally stimulates the Kundalini into activity, which becomes, so to say, "fired," and aroused into action. As this energy passes up the spine it stimulates in turn the various psychic centers, causing them to glow and spring into activity; and as this occurs the various psychic faculties automatically come into being.

(Among the psychic faculties which the Yogi claims to possess are: the ability to leave the physical body; the power to prolong life or to die at will; the ability to control dreams; the ability to read the thoughts of others; the ability to perceive events at a distance; the ability to levitate the human body and walk upon water, and so on.)

The Prana is thought to be circulated throughout the body by means of a number of etheric channels or conductors known as the Nadis; and when a certain stage in the breathing exercises has been reached an internal sound is heard, known as "The Voice of the Nada."

There are two main breaths, known respectively as the Sun and Moon breaths. One of these passes through the right nostril, the other through the left. Symbolically they are represented by the rivers Ganges and Jumna; and the spot between the eyebrows is known as Benares, the sacred city. So that, to the Hindus, Benares represents not only the sacred city itself, but also this secret, psychic center.

There are twenty-four principal modes of breathing, involving largely changes from the right to the left nostril, and vice versa.

What are known as Mudras are postures assumed by the Yogi, in which the correct Asana is assumed, while practicing Pranayama and meditation. Of these Mudras the Yoni Mudra is the first step in Laya Yoga. When assuming it, the left finger is lifted from the left nostril and Prana inhaled through it; then exhaled through the right nostril.

Four stages are involved: (1) piercing the ganthis (knots); (2) inducing rhythm of the nerve currents; (3) directing the breath toward the pineal gland; and (4) the hearing of the "soundless sound."

The Vajroli Mudra is among the most secret of all, involving much material which cannot be given outside a medical treatise. Fluid is drawn up into the body through the urethra. This cultivated ability is utilized in certain physical practices, the male and female fluidic essences being imbibed in this manner during sexual intercourse. Virya and Raja are combined, drawn into the body and there retained. This is one of the most closely guarded of all the secrets of Yoga.

We now come to a few lesser-known principles regarding these esoteric doctrines. The Yoga practices, which are said to be some five thousand years old, seek primarily, as we have said, the attainment of cosmic consciousness, or union with the absolute. In order to accomplish this the human mind must not only be stilled but, so to say, disposed of altogether.

It has been said that, in Yoga, we "see the fountain and not the flow," meaning that the *source* of consciousness is perceived, rather than consciousness itself.

Music is vibration, and the Mantras embody certain forms of vibration which are thought to be especially potent. It is the accentuation of the words, rather than the words themselves, which is important, and it is held that the influence of many of these Mantras is enormous.

Aum and Aum Mani Padme Hum we have already mentioned. One powerful Mantram is Soham, meaning "I am He." It means union with the universal consciousness. The Mantram Hansa is also well known, and was discussed in some detail by Mme. Blavatsky. When we exhale, the breath passes with the sound *Ha,* and enters with the sound *Sa.* Combined we have Hansa.

(Hatha Yoga deals essentially with the body and is derived from the words *Ha* [sun] and *Tha* [moon]. It represents a combination of the Sun and Moon breaths before mentioned. The breath entering the right nostril is said to be warm and positive, while that entering the left nostril is cold and negative.)

We now come to a few of the special postures.

Let us first consider Sidhasana. In this posture the left heel is pressed against the perineum, and the right heel against the front of the body directly before it. The hands are placed on the knees, with the thumbs and first fingers joined, the spine being erect. If the chin be pressed tightly against the throat, the senses restrained, and the inner gaze fixed on the spot between the eyebrows, "absolute freedom" is said to be ultimately attained.

In the Virasana posture, the right foot is placed under the right thigh and the left foot under the left thigh. The feet are kept flat and the hands are rested on the thighs, the palms overlapping each other.

In the Paschimatana posture, the legs and feet are kept straight in front of the body, the toes being clasped by the hands—the body being bent forward for this purpose.

In the Metsyendrasana posture, which is used for changing the psychic currents in the body, the right heel is pressed against the navel, while the left leg is crossed to the right, bringing the left heel to the right knee. Then the right arm is crossed, turning the head and body toward the back, and the toe of the left foot is held with the right hand. The toe of the left foot is now grasped with the left hand from the back.

In the Dhyanasana posture, the right foot is tucked under the armpit on the right side, the left leg is bent crosswise and the hands clasped over the left knee.

Over and over again, in Hatha Yoga practices, it is emphasized that the body must be purified before these exercises can be attempted with safety. Here we return to our preliminaries—Yama and Niyama. Various special procedures are however undertaken in order to insure this purification. One of these is known as Neti, and consists in passing an unraveled piece of cord or yarn through the nose and throat and pulling it back and forth. In Dhouti a strip of cloth is swallowed and then pulled up again. In Basti the lower bowel is washed out with water, drawn into it by muscular action. In Trataka the practitioner stares at a lighted candle until tears come into his eyes. In Naulica the lower intestines are rolled about, after drawing the water into them. In Kapalabhati rapid breathing is undertaken like a pair of bellows—the spine being held erect. All of these are accompanied by special modes of breathing.

Khecheri may be likened to hibernation or suspended animation. In this, as in all these exercises, the realization of the Self is assisted through these special, physical, preliminary exercises.

The percentage of consciousness and unconsciousness (the latter being called the inactive condition of consciousness) is said to be approximately as follows:

Hibernation of a frog or turtle: five per cent consciousness and ninety-five per cent unconsciousness.

YOGA AND MAGIC

The seedless trance of the yogi: ninety-five per cent consciousness and five per cent unconsciousness.

Between these two extremes there are said to be twelve stages. Objective consciousness, or consciousness of the world, is the inflow, while subjective consciousness, or the awareness of Self, is the outflow.

There are seven degrees of consciousness, ranging from the deepest sleep to the highest form of meditation by the Yogi.

In Susupti, or deep sleep, we have fifteen per cent active and eighty-five per cent inactive consciousness. (Sleep is in turn divided into three stages [1] ordinary sleep; [2] animal sleep or mesmerism; and [3] deep sleep.)

In Swapna we find a state of dream, in which there is twenty-five per cent active and seventy-five per cent inactive consciousness.

In Jagrata we have the normal, waking conscious life. This in turn is divided into (1) Mudha, blank wakefulness, and (2) Ksipta, a wandering state of mind, as in uncontrolled imagination.

In mediumistic trance there is said to be forty-five per cent active and fifty-five per cent inactive consciousness. In Vicharana we have constructive thinking and imagination, in which there is fifty-five per cent active and forty-five per cent inactive consciousness.

In Ekagrata we have one-pointedness of mind, as in concentration, embodying seventy per cent active and thirty per cent inactive consciousness.

In Dhyanastha, embodying finer concentration or deep meditation, we have eighty per cent active and twenty per cent inactive consciousness. In this state the molecules of the "mental body" are said to be thrown into a high state of vibration and become rhythmical. Great calm is experienced as the consciousness expands.

In Turyaga higher self-consciousness is attained, together with unity, and in this state ninety per cent consciousness and ten per cent unconsciousness is manifest.

(Higher states of consciousness are said to be attained by various poets and mystics *spontaneously,* due to the rhythmic words or Mantras which they employ in their poetry—as in the cases of Tennyson, Whitman and others.)

There are three stages of Samadhi: (1) The seeded trance; (2) the seedless trance, and (3) the perfect trance. In the seeded trance a definite object of concentration is kept before the mind. In seedless trance this is obliterated, but the mind nevertheless does not become negative or inactive. In perfect trance, union with the absolute consciousness is attained.

In the second stage of trance the lower bodies are forgotten (not left). In the highest trance, on the other hand, they are *left*—that is, the Yogi may "die," but voluntarily. He has attained union.

We know the world through the senses first, then through the mind; finally through these higher psychic faculties. Joy, which is the object of life, is not strictly speaking an object, such as a child, but exists in the mind.

One enters into the mind of another person by understanding his nature, and this in turn is attained through the various Mudras. Such contact is part of the fuller realization of Self; and it must be remembered that the object of life consists mainly in this self-realization.

None of these Yoga practices can be understood unless the point of view of the Yogi is first of all apprehended, which is that everything in the universe is but the expression of ultimate oneness—that is, absolute consciousness. We are but fragments of this universal consciousness, and the realization of this fact leads automatically to unifica-

YOGA AND MAGIC

tion with it, which is the object of all these Yoga practices.

Tibetan Yoga

While many of these Indian exercises are difficult in the extreme, those undertaken by the ascetics in Tibet are more rigid still—and it must be remembered that these are followed in a climate which is for the most part bitterly cold and forbidding. Many of these forms of Tibetan Yoga have of late years been expounded quite fully in the books of Alexandra David-Neal, Dr. W. Y. Evans-Wentz, and others, so that they may be summarized very briefly here.

One of the most rigid—indeed terrible—of these ascetic practices is known as Tsams, in which the Yogi lives forever alone, in complete darkness, in utter isolation from the world. Year after year he lives on, seeing nothing, never a ray of light reaching him, his food being placed outside his door by other hands. In this lonely darkness he practices meditation—often, no doubt, ending in madness.

Another terrible form of ascetic development is known as Chod, in which the physical body (often symbolically) is theoretically given over to demons or animals, in order that spiritual "enlightenment" may ensue. From our point of view these extreme mortifications can only be regarded as abnormal perversions of true psychic development.

The Tibetans, however, regard these practices according to another light. The only way we can achieve any understanding of the motive behind them is by understanding the fundamental concept of Buddhism. A fundamental tenet is the doctrine of Anatta—that is to say, of egolessness. The very basis upon which most of us construct our lives is a falsehood. The ego is only a phenomenon. It has no final reality. It is just as illusory as our perception of the rising of the sun in the east, and of the whirling past us of the landscape when we stare from the window of a train traveling fifty miles an hour. The Tibetan Yogi, therefore, attempts to eradicate this false notion of self. So, in this ceremony of Chod, he deliberately gives his body, his feelings and his mind to whoever will take them, so that in this way he may achieve a realization of "the essence of mind which is intrinsically pure," behind the phenomena of body and mind and the whole illusory world. So, to pay his debt to the life-process which he has defiled by his egocentric belief, he gives "my flesh to the hungry, my blood to the thirsty, my skin to clothe those who are naked, my bones as fuel to those who suffer from cold. I give my happiness to the unhappy ones. I give my breath to bring back the dying to life."

It is thus an idealized form of personal sacrifice, of giving up everything that one is and has, to the rest of life. The celebrated traveler, Mme. Alexandra David-Neal, describes this sacrifice in typically Buddhist terms. "He must realize that the very idea of sacrifice is but an illusion, an offshoot of blind, groundless pride. In fact, he has nothing to give away because he is nothing. These useless bones, symbolizing the destruction of his phantom 'I' may sink into the muddy lake; it will not matter. That silent renunciation of the ascetic who realizes that he holds nothing that he can renounce, and who utterly relinquishes the elation springing from the idea of sacrifice, closes the right."

A special Mantram is in common use among Tibetan Yogis: Hik. . . . Phat! This Mantram is said to be enormously powerful, even to the extent of releasing the spirit from the body.

Parvos are Tibetan mediums, and they speak quite

YOGA AND MAGIC

naturally of Delogs—people of the astral. They also write at length of Angkur, empowerment, which consists in giving energy or power to another person or thing— much as our mediums have been known to transfer their psychic power to others, or to inanimate objects on occasion. They also write extensively of Mong Jug, which signifies the translation of the soul from one body to another —a form of living "possession."

Two methods of psychic development seem peculiar to the Tibetans: Lung Gom, which consists in the ability to run long distances without fatigue, and seemingly without normal contact with the ground, by means of certain specific breathing exercises; and Tumo, which is the creation within the body of extraordinary internal heat, by which it is warmed, even in the bitterest weather.

A brief description of this latter procedure may be of interest, since it enables the ascetic to live, entirely naked, in the bitterest cold of the Tibetan winter.

The ascetic sits on the ground, or on a mat, crosslegged in the proper Asana. He must eat nothing before undertaking the exercises. The mind is calmed and centered, and the essential breathing exercises begun.

A golden Lotus is imagined on a level with the navel; on it is the Sanskrit character Rm (Ram). Above Ram is Ma, from which the goddess Dorjee Naljorma emerges. The Self is identified with the latter. A magic letter, A, on the navel, is visualized, and Ha at the top of the head. There is a fire in A.

By means of slow, deep inhalations, the fire in A is fanned into a flame (by retention of the breath, etc.). This fire slowly ascends the Nadis (psychic veins).

This fire is first of all imagined as the size of a thread; then as big as the finger; then as big as the arm; then as big as the whole body; then as a sea of fire. Toward the end of the meditation this procedure is reversed, until it again becomes only as large as a thread. This is then followed by a period of meditation. Thus is Tumo practiced. By its means, it is said, the Yogi is enabled to withstand the bitterest cold, and to live entirely without covering in the severest snowstorms. He has created internal heat sufficient to withstand them.

Many of these Tibetan practices, it should be observed, border on magic. Ceremonies and invocations are performed, and their whole system is evidently a curious mixture of higher psychical development and black magic of a low order. Let us now see what connections there may be between some of these Tantrik and Tibetan rituals, and magic, as practiced by occidental magicians in the middle ages.

Ceremonial Magic

It has been said that the so-called occult sciences may be divided into six branches. These may again be classified under three headings. The first of these, dealing with the occult properties of nature, includes magic and alchemy. The second, pneumatology, includes divination, sorcery and demonology. The third—and perhaps the most ancient of all—is astrology.

Alchemy is of course the precursor of chemistry, just as astrology is the precursor of astronomy; while the other branches would constitute the remote ancestors of modern psychical research.

The word magic is usually associated in the public mind with evil or black magic; but as a matter of fact the latter is but an illegitimate offshoot of the original science (white magic), which consisted in the occult utilization of the subtle forces of nature for beneficent purposes.

YOGA AND MAGIC

Magic has indeed a venerable history. Aside from the oriental nations, magic originated in Assyria and Chaldea, being also independently developed in Egypt. Here the magical arts were cultivated assiduously. The various portions of the human body were dedicated by the Egyptians to their respective gods: to Ra, the head; to Anubis, the nose and lips; Hathor, the eyes; to Selk, the teeth, and so on. Hekate, the moon goddess, was the patron-divinity of sorcerers. The attribution of these gods to different parts of the human body bears a striking resemblance to the mythical physiology of the Yogis described above, where each Chakra contains a letter of the Sanskrit alphabet, a certain current of force and a deity.

Not only does the Chakra contain a letter, but it also bears within it the name of the deity and certain specific spiritual words. An accumulation of these words and letters weave themselves into the Mantras, which are analogous to the invocations and incantations of magical repute. If we turn to the classical invocations of Greek and medieval times, we find many curious and barbarous words, perplexing to the mind, and baffling so far as concerns their origin. Among them were: Aski, Kataski, Haix, Tetraz, Damnameneus and Sision. These words were used to exorcise or clean places of evil repute, and to drive away demons. Abracadabra (or Abrahadabra), mentioned by O. Seranus Ammoniacus in his *De Medic.*, circa 53 A.D., was, according to him, compounded of three Hebrew words, meaning "a father," "a spirit," and "a word." It was said to be one of the most sacred of all names, and a great word of power.

Sacred names and words are used in all invocations, among them the powerful tetragrammaton. Words of power employed by the modern magician (really ancient) are Abraxas, Xnoubis, Meithras, Abracadabra, and others.

There is of course an enormous literature on the subject of magic, to which it would be impossible even to refer. Let us rather summarize very briefly some of the views expressed by modern scientific magicians, in our twentieth century, and see what they may have to say upon the subject.

"The object of the magical ritual is the unification of the macrocosm with the microcosm." This of course at once reminds us of the unification with the absolute, as set forth in the Yoga teachings.

All the above is not too dissimilar to the various goals established by the practitioners of Yoga. But here our resemblance ends. However difficult it may be for us to comprehend the rationale of Yoga, nevertheless we can discern a certain method and technique which does not strain too greatly our power of understanding. But the technique of magic is a totally different story. For here we are confronted by technical processes and procedures in which there is no similarity to anything in our background. When the practitioner of magic speaks of gods, invocation, body of light, clairvoyance, or skrying in the spirit vision, we are a little dazed by the bewildering complexity of these strange notions. This is because magic is based upon an understanding of a world order which is thoroughly different from our western scientific one. The magus theoretically postulates the existence of a divine order in and behind the physical world, rather as does the Yogi when he speaks of Chakras, Pranas, Vayus and Purushas existing in the human body, unseen by us.

Although this concept seems fantastic, nevertheless the magus is above all practical. When, for example, in bacteriology the causative agent of a disease is suspected to

YOGA AND MAGIC

be a virus, scientific effort at once applies itself to the practical consideration of devising means and instruments whereby the morphology, characteristics, and cultural peculiarities of the virus may be better perceived and understood. Likewise the magus attempts to develop within himself the apparatus required for the investigation of the super-physical world which he believes in.

Possibly the most outstanding of his instruments is the so-called body of light. There are various ways of understanding this even among the magicians themselves. Some believe in the real objective existence within the human body of an inner body, invisible to us normally because of being composed of very fine subtle electrical substance. Others regard the body of light as an imaginative formulation of oneself in the world of mind so as to be able to explore the hidden world of mind. By the constant use of this body of light, a supersensory faculty of clairvoyance is said to develop.

The proper way to develop clairvoyance, according to the magicians, is to "develop the body of light until it is just as real as the physical body, and teach it to travel to any desired symbol, and to enable it to perform all necessary rites and invocations—in short, to educate it."

In order to cultivate this ability, the magician should begin by imagining himself outside his physical body, standing in front of himself; then transfer his consciousness to the astral body, so that he can see with its eyes, hear with its ears, and so forth. In short, he should seek to attain conscious and voluntary astral projection.

The experimenter is warned, however, to project himself at first only within the boundary of the magic circle, which has previously been consecrated and is thus safe. By performing such rituals as the pentagram and hexagram rituals and by circumambulating the circle, the psychic energy is kept within it and is used by the magician in much the same way as a spiritualist medium is said to use the energy of sitters within her circle. When practicing astral projection, according to the magical rituals, it is important to bring the double back properly before terminating the experiment, otherwise there may be unpleasant psychic complications.

By exercising the astral body constantly it becomes strengthened, and also learns a sense of direction. The sincere magician will take the magical eucharist often, thus feeding and renewing his spiritual body. Veiled allusions to all this, and to magical transformations, may be found in the Egyptian *Book of the Dead.*

To what extent do modern magicians believe in the efficacy of such rites, rituals, invocations and ceremonies? To what extent would they ascribe the results obtained to objective phenomena or to subjective experience? Various replies to these questions have been made. Many magicians contend that the main object of all such rites is to "inflame the mind," thus insuring success in invocations. The effects, then, would be mainly psychological, even physiological, in the last analysis.

The theory underlying the use of invocation with its supposed goal of exaltation can well be explained by what we know to be true today. Many critics dismiss magic and its invocations with the simple retort of "auto-suggestion." But we know that there are innumerable difficulties attending the successful use of self-suggestion. Thousands of people have attempted to give themselves suggestions about health, their life-relations, faculties of mind, and so on, without any perceptible results occurring. The reason for this is not difficult to see. The person employing auto-suggestion is attempting to drop constructive ideas into the deep levels of his subconscious

YOGA AND MAGIC

mind, which is, so psychology would tell us, the dynamic and creative part of the mind. So that, if the suggestion manages to seep through that obstinate barrier that divides the human psyche, blotting out all awareness of what goes on underneath, then the individual may well expect truly magical results. The great difficulty, as already discovered, is to get behind this barrier. Many solutions have been broached. These range all the way from sitting in a dimly-lighted room, relaxing the body, listening to soft quiet music, concentration, to an interminable repetition of suggestions or affirmations. As said, these are none too successful.

It seems as though those responsible for the creation of magic realized this difficulty. They knew that the suggestions contained within the rituals—"I am he, the bornless spirit," "I see by mine own inward light," "I am he who is clothed with a body of flesh, yet in whom flames the spirit of the eternal gods"—stood very little chance of penetrating the subconscious mind unless some mechanism could be devised, either of increasing enormously the potency of the suggestions or else of temporarily disrupting the censorship of this barrier intervening between the mind and the subconscious.

Both methods therefore were used. Their suggestions were clothed in religious terminology so as to obtain the religious and moral reinforcement that such terminology contains. And secondly, they devised a whole series of mechanisms to overcome the impenetrability of the supposed barrier between the two levels of the psyche by resorting to chanting, long prayers, barbarous words of evocation, which excited the mind by their mysteriousness and their senselessness, by tracing lineal figures and sigils in the air, by employing celebrations akin to the eucharist, and by wearing bright and differently colored gowns, costumes and robes. The *tout ensemble* of all these adjuncts, if properly performed, would so stimulate the mind as to exalt the individual above and beyond his normal capacity into a strange kind of frenzy. It is this frenzy, or this ecstasy, which insures the success of invocation. Under such conditions, it is imperative for the suggestion to move in but one direction—into the depths of the subconscious.

One rule is powerfully enunciated by the magicians. What we today call the subconscious can be reached only by two processes—either by intense concentration, which was the method employed by the Yogis, or by an emotional crisis or orgasm, which was the method adopted in magical technique.

Another school of magicians, however, contend that the gods, angels and spirits, invoked by the magical rites, are no mere figments of the imagination, no simple hallucinations constructed around the thought of a suggestion, but are objective in a thoroughgoing manner. All schools, however, agree that there are exoteric and esoteric meanings in all the above—just as there were in Alchemy—for the alchemists were everything from chemists to spiritual mystics.

Truth, the modern magician says, can be ascertained only by realizing the unity which lies beyond and behind all phenomena, and which replaces the illusory duality of the human mind. Unity transcends consciousness, for the mind is by nature dual; but magic can unify the consciousness, thus including all things; and it is this unity which it attained by the right magical practices. . . . In all the above, it will be observed, magic closely resembles the union of Yoga; and these interesting analogies could be greatly expanded. Such would be the esoteric meanings, as opposed to the crude, exoteric significances attached

YOGA AND MAGIC

to it by many modern magicians. It is to be hoped that these points of analogy may one day be pointed out in detail by someone who has the necessary time, patience and knowledge to do so, based upon a thorough knowledge of the literature of all these subjects. The necessity of connecting these teachings with modern, scientific psychology need hardly be emphasized. The field here is a vast and interesting one, and it is to be hoped that some young and enterprising psychologist of the future will some day undertake it!

APPENDIX

ON SOME POSSIBLE RELATIONS BETWEEN PSYCHICAL RESEARCH AND OTHER SCIENCES

INASMUCH AS ALL true scientific explanation consists in dovetailing the unknown into the known, and showing their possible relationships, it is important to show such connections between psychical research and the other sciences, if possible, and to suggest ideas for further study along these lines. But little has been done in this direction. The nearest approach to what I have in mind is Dr. A. Marques' book *Scientific Corroborations of Theosophy*. This book is however limited to the relationship between the purely theosophic doctrines and modern scientific data, and does not enter the more general field. The following is a brief summary of possible analogies and lines for future research:

Biology: Relationship between the Yoga teachings, as to the Chakras, the Kundalini, and so on, to physiological teachings, the nervous plexuses, the ductless glands, and so on. Possible nervous centers and currents in the human body. Vital radiations. Respiration, in relation to the Yoga teachings regarding Prana. Is mental energy an energy? Is moral energy an energy? (See in this connection Ostwald's *Theory of Energetics,* and Dr. Hartmann's booklet *The Correlation of Spiritual Forces.*) Various rays said to come from the human body. The human aura. Thought-photography. Magnetism from the hands; relation to healings. Perfumes and scents. Genius possibly dependent upon a subtle internal secretion. (See

Equinox, Vol. 9.) Telepathic transfer of smells and tastes. Power of the mind over the body. Stigmata. The action of drugs on consciousness. Sex, in relation to poltergeist phenomena and to the Yoga teachings. Cases of transference of psychic power, as with Home and Palladino. Transference of sensibility. Exteriorization of motivity and sensibility. Death and phenomena associated with it (psychical and physiological). The consciousness of dying. Visions of the dying. Study of fasting cases. Clinical studies of mediums, by means of instruments of precision. (See *Laboratory Investigations into Psychic Phenomena.*)

Chemistry: Alchemy. So-called "occult chemistry." Fire. (See Wadia's *Message of Zoroaster.*) Incense and perfumes. Psychic scents at séances. Chemical tests used for psychic investigation.

Physics: Vital radiations from the body. Electroscope discharged without contact. Instrumental tests of mediums. Dr. Crawford's theory of table levitations. Weighing tests with scales. Connection with theory of gravity. Ultra-violet and infra-red rays. Darkness and light. Possible energy common to two worlds. Cold breezes felt at séances. Registration of the same. Atmospheric electricity. The problem of so-called "apports."

Mathematics: Theory of the Fourth Dimension, as applied to psychic phenomena (Zöllner). Chance coincidence in psychic research.

Psychology, Normal and Abnormal: (See *Psychology in the Light of Psychic Phenomena.*) Possibility of a superconscious. The question of so-called obsession. Possible psychic factor in certain forms of insanity. Trance. The action of various drugs. Psychotherapy.

Anthropology: The necessity of studying psychic phenomena among primitive peoples, sympathetically. (See **The Psychic World.**)

INDEX

ALLEN, Dr. Thomas G., 30
ARISTOTLE, 52

BABSON, Roger W., 16
BAGGALLY, W. W., 27
BALLET, M., 92
BARADUC, Dr. H., 95
BERGEN, Eddie, 71
BERGSON, Henri, 92, 153
BLAVATSKY, Mme., 171
BOTTAZZI, Prof., 53
BROAD, C. D., 157
BUGUET, Edouard, 121

CARREL, Dr. Alexis, 10, 106
CARTHEUSER, William, 64, 68-93
CHARPENTIER, Prof., 92
CLIFFORD, W. K., 144
COURTIER, Jules, 92
CRAWFORD, W. J., 187
CROOKES, Sir William, 31, 40, 53
CURIE, M. & Mme., 92

D'ARC, Jeanne, 135-39
D'ARSONVAL, M., 92
DAVID-NEAL, Alexandre, 175, 176
DEANE, Mrs. Ada E., 121
DUFF, Rev. Edward M., 30
DUGUID, David, 121
DUNNE, J. W., 157

EDWARDS, Dawn, 8, 74
EVANS-WENTZ, W. Y., 175

FALCONER, brothers, 121
FEILDING, Hon. Everard, 27
FODOR, Dr. Nandor, 101, 120

FROHMAN, Daniel, 37

GARRETT, Mrs. Eileen, 50, 59-63, 67
GASKELL, Mrs., 99
GATES, Dr. Elmer, 108
GOËTHE, 151
GÜRWITSCH, 99

HARTMANN, Dr. Franz, 186
HODGSON, Dr. Richard, 41, 42, 43, 49, 50, 51
HOME, D. D., 53, 87, 187
HOPE, William, 121
HOPPER, B. J., 101
HUXLEY, 143-44
HYSLOP, Dr. James H., 43, 44, 49

JAMES, Prof. William, 12, 41, 42, 43, 142
JOHNSTON, Dr. William B., 95, 102
JUNG, Dr. Carl G., 60

KANT, 143
KEELER, William M., 121
KILNER, Dr. Walter J., 107

LACEY, Thomas, 64-8, 89
LANG, Andrew, 138
LEAF, Dr. Walter, 42
LEONARD, Mrs. Osborne, 51
LODGE, Sir Oliver, 31, 37, 42
LOMBROSO, Cesar, 33
LOWELL, Percival, 145

MACDOUGALL, Dr. Duncan, 94
McCOMUS, Prof. Henry C., 75, 81

INDEX

McDougall, Prof. William, 143, 147
Margery, 64
Marques, Dr. A., 186
Moore, Vice-Admiral, 79
Mumler, William H., 121
Myers, F. W. H., 158
Myers, John, 121

Newton, 151

Ostwald, Wilhelm, 186
Osty, Dr. Eugène, 53, 54, 55

Palladino, Eusapia, 27-40, 53, 87, 89, 187
Piper, Mrs. Leonore E., 41-51
Podmore, Frank, 110
Price, Harry, 18, 57, 120, 124
Price, Prof. H. H., 157

Rahn, Prof. Otto, 99
Regardie, Dr. F. I., 8
Rhine, Dr. J. B., 11, 89
Richet, Prof. Charles, 47, 92
Romains, Jules, 10

Saltmarsh, H. F., 154, 157

Schneider, Willie & Rudi, 53, 54, 55
Schrenck-Notzing, Dr. von, 86-7
Seabrook, William B., 158
Sidgwick, Prof. Henry, 42
Silverberg, W., 77, 79, 88, 91
Socrates, 9-10, 137
Spencer, Herbert, 143
Spinoza, 143
Steinmetz, Charles P., 16
Stella, C., 53
Stümpf, Prof., 143

Tennyson, 174
Thurston, Howard, 32-3
Tilford, Frank, 37

Wadia, Dr., 187
Watters, Dr. R. A., 95, 100-1, 102, 104
Whitman, Walt, 174
Wilson, C. T. R., 98

X, Miss, 18

Zimmer, Ernst, 153
Zöllner, Prof., 187